Designing
Your Happiness

A Contemporary Look at
Feng Shui

Designing
Your Happiness

A Contemporary Look at
Feng Shui

Nancilee Wydra

**You and Your Living Space,
A New Partnership**

HEIAN

To those who have nurtured my dreams.

© 1995 Nancilee Wydra
© 1995 illustrations by Seita Kabashima and Kazue Sakurai
© 1995 cover design by Lydia Nienart
loupan image derived from **Feng Shui** by E. Eitel, Graham Brash
Author's photo by Suzan Phillips

First Edition 1995
95 96 97 98 99 00 10 9 8 7 6 5 4 3 2 1

Heian International, Inc.
1815 W. 205th St. Suite #301
Torrance, CA 90501

ISBN# 0-89346-811-8

Printed in the United States of America

Contents

Part II:

Part I

Introduction

When was the last time you moved? Each year millions of people will undergo that ordeal. Choosing a neighborhood, selecting a dwelling and arranging furniture can bring a sane person to the brink of hysteria. One needs patience, fortitude and a sense of humor to sift through the mountains of real estate ads and walk through legions of square footage to find a place that speaks to one's soul. Even after our pocketbooks and desires mesh, enabling us to select a dwelling, we find ourselves embroiled in what feels like a battle without an opponent. We struggle to shape a house into a home with only glossy magazine pictures and amorphous childhood memories to guide us. Left afloat in a sea of confusion and lacking much knowledge, we try to sort out what makes us feel good.

1977 was my year to search for a new place to live. After wrestling with the demons of "I want" and "I should", I selected a five acre parcel of land overlooking a stream. It had the privacy I yearned for at a price tag I could afford. Sounds too good to be true? It was. The structure I would call home was fraught with challenges. It was a converted one-car garage with an outhouse. But my instincts pulled me toward this site. Its siren call lured me to a seemingly reckless choice. Taking a quantum leap over more rational alternatives, I purchased it.

My home in 1977

In spite of the hardships that came with this territory, I did indeed thrive. My instincts were on target. Family, health and work flourished while I lived there. A successful career and its attendant monetary rewards gave me the muscle to transform this ragamuffin into royalty. Many years and nine additions later, this formerly one-room dwelling became my dream home.

My home now

Just about the time the last nail was being hammered into the final addition, I discovered feng shui. This ancient Chinese discipline showed me how the physical environment can have a dramatic impact on the course of one's life. I learned that the location of a home, and the placement of its furniture, lighting, and accessories all affect a person's potential happiness. Feng shui validated my instincts.

The Chinese claim that success and failure in life are often linked to the home. With a knowledge of feng shui you can choose:

1. a lucky building site;
2. the best way to position a house on a building lot;
3. an auspicious way to arrange furniture.

The belief systems that shaped feng shui are the same ones that gave rise to acupuncture, herbal medicine, martial arts and macrobiotic diets.

Over time I came to realize that one's habitat is as integral to self-actualization as is the genetic coding in our DNA. When we discover how to situate ourselves in our environment, we unleash additional personal power for our lives. The more I learned about feng shui, the more apparent it became that our living environment can either assist or thwart us in directing our lives toward success.

The ability to recognize and correct a problem in one's living space in a manner that will augment the realization of personal goals provides us with additional fuel for our journey through life. Since a home's environment can increase the chances of achieving and maintaining health, becoming financially successful, and having satisfying interpersonal relationships, it makes sense to examine the teachings of feng shui. It worked for me. This book will show you how to make it work for you.

How to Pronounce Feng Shui

One day, before hearing feng shui discussed in the media or by any knowledgeable person, I was discussing the captivating subject with a group of women friends. One friend, who happened to be Chinese, balked at my erroneous pronunciation of "phen chewy (sic)."

She hastened to enlighten me that the best way for our Western mouths to articulate these Chinese sounds is something like this.

Feng rhymes with tongue   FONGUE
Shui rhymes with sway   SCHWAY

The voice lowers as it says "fongue" and extends the word "schway" in a seemingly endless manner.

3

Chapter One

Discover Feng Shui

Why Learn About Feng Shui?

How does your home make you feel? Are you nurtured and energized when you walk through your front door? If your home heightens a sense of well-being, can you determine why? Is it the comfort of a favorite chair, morning sunlight pouring through a kitchen window or potted plants adorning a window sill? Conversely, why do some places make you feel uneasy? Could it be the absence of natural lighting, a narrow hallway, or clutter that assaults your sense of well-being? Learning about feng shui will help you to discover why some places radiate either a sense of well-being or a feeling of discomfort.

For more than 2,000 years, the Chinese have used the teachings of feng shui, a system that correlates health, prosperity, and good luck with many factors in a living environment. It is as central to Chinese culture as the Bill of Rights is to ours. When choosing a home, it is unlikely that a Chinese family would ignore feng shui considerations just as we would seldom neglect to secure a legal closing document. The Chinese believe that the street one lives on, the layout of one's home and the placement of its furnishings all play a key role in promoting good health, maintaining satisfying relationships and achieving financial success.

Success, good luck and fortune are interactive concepts which are not bestowed upon us but, instead, are dynamically sought. Feng shui allows us to place ourselves in the best position possible to be available to good luck. We can attract or deter success through our deeds, our efforts and our place on this earth. Moreover, we are responsible for contributing to the greater good and in so doing it will be reflected back to us.

Many of our memories include a sense of place. When we reminisce about our childhood, we can often picture where we were and how we felt about our surroundings. My husband grew up in a large family. Each family member reminisces with great affection about life at "the cottage". They had lived in other locations, but this one has emerged as the most memorable. The cottage probably "felt good" because it embraced certain ideals basic to feng shui. It was situated mid-way up a hill, it faced southeast, and it overlooked a pristine body of water. Once you've learned more about feng shui, you'll understand why these features are considered fortunate.

Certain universal conditions contribute to making a place feel good, and feng shui clearly defines specific conditions. Although we some- times spend considerable time and effort attempting to optimize our health, relationships and careers, we often overlook the influence of our surroundings on our lives. We use the word decorate, which Webster's Dictionary defines as "to furnish or adorn with something ornamental", to describe how we organize our dwellings. Designing our living space in this way, according to feng shui, is as off base as purchasing stylish clothes in order to stay healthy.

Feng shui can help to take the guesswork out of decision making. You will be able to choose the best place to live, the correct location for a sofa, or the luckiest room in which to work with a basic knowledge of feng shui.

What is Feng Shui?

In the simplest terms, feng shui posits that our accomplishments in life are influenced by the places where we live and work. Feng shui investigates the influences of topography, vegetation, water sources, site plans, floor plans, furniture placement, colors, architectural details and neighborhoods on our lives. When conditions are not ideal, feng shui suggests ways in which to make improvements.

Placement is the key to good fortune. If your bed faces east toward a window, you are greeted each morning by a lighter, brighter world than if the bed faced west. Sunlight makes us feel more optimistic and happy, and these feelings help to elevate our daily performance. Like the tentacles of an octopus, one's attitude has far-reaching consequences.

According to feng shui, most imperfect conditions can be remedied or cured. Feng shui can provide solutions to such questions as:

Health - What factors in my home contribute to headaches? How can I ease stomach problems? Why am I susceptible to back problems?

Relationships - How can I attract a mate? Why do my children argue at the dinner table? How can I cultivate a better relationship with my boss?

Career/Self-actualization - Why have I been bypassed for promotion? How can I awaken my creativity? How can I arrange my office or store to improve business?

While some areas require more adjustment than others, most can be altered to foster good fortune. The ways to cure ills can be as diverse as women's fashions. Feng shui is an art, not a science, and it reflects the fashions of time and place. Although universal human needs are addressed, one must always acknowledge a culture's particular world view. Thus, the original ancient Chinese interpretations must be reviewed in light of 20th century Western realities, for without integrating contemporary ideas into feng shui's body of knowledge, it appears archaic.

For example, many Chinese use principles of feng shui to determine appropriate grave sites for family members. According to the Chinese, a properly placed grave can affect a family's future; thus a great deal of time is devoted to this issue. However, with today's land use constraints, the scattering of family members and the option of cremation, Westerners are less concerned about the physical location of a burial site.

Feng shui is more than the sum of its parts. It evokes in us a new attitude and a new way of viewing our living spaces as an integral part of our total experience.

7

How Feng Shui Works

Before Feng Shui can help you, you must first identify the problem you want solved. In my first year as a feng shui consultant, I was asked to help a client with weight control. Although it seemed like a problem for a nutritionist, I decided to consider this issue from a feng shui perspective. I asked her to describe to me **where** she ate and **when** she ate. The following tale unfolded.

Upon arriving home from work each day, she was drawn to the contents of her refrigerator like steel to a magnet. And it didn't end there. Television commercials and moments between chores justified taking a "refrigerator break". Moreover, these mini-meals weren't dignified by sitting down at a table; rather they were consumed quick as a wink while she stood at the refrigerator.

With these facts in mind, I uncovered the problem in her kitchen. Upon entering, one was greeted by an unobstructed pathway to the refrigerator, and the refrigerator door seemed to beckon to all who entered. No more than three unimpeded steps were needed to traverse the distance between the kitchen entrance and the refrigerator door. This direct path was not the answer for someone who was trying to avoid overeating!

Feng shui regards as negative any path that encourages or allows swift passage because energy (also known as "ch'i") moves along that path too quickly. Walkways should curve or have some visual interruptions along the way to help moderate the flow of ch'i.

Interrupting the path to the refrigerator and providing distractions along the way was the feng shui "cure" I suggested.

First we placed the kitchen table in the center of the room to interrupt the direct pathway. We hoped that it would slow her down enough to consider the consequences of going to the refrigerator. Secondly, I asked her to place such enjoyable diversions as unsolved crossword puzzles and magazines on the table. These pleasant alternatives could help strengthen her resolve and bolster her will power.

What You Already Know About Feng Shui

On an intuitive level, you already know a great deal about feng shui. Consider the following question.

In a traditional classroom, where do the better students usually sit?

a) Near the exit door.
b) Near the front of the room.
c) Near a bank of windows.

You may have selected "b" just as the better students do when they choose to sit in the front of the classroom. After all, the nearer you are to a source of energy the more likely it is that you will absorb its benefits. The closer you are to a fireplace, the warmer you will feel. And, since the teacher is the source from which learning is transmitted, those who sit in the front of the room are more likely to absorb the lesson.

There is often a preferred location that allows the attainment of desired results. Consider the many appropriate ways in which your instincts are already guiding you. Sitting close to a teacher, waking up facing the rising sun, facing the entrance door of your office--all are locations that will influence your performance. Learning to position yourself in any situation to help realize your goals is one of feng shui's benefits.

Feng shui does not, however, concern itself with style. Taste is related to time and place. The large, over-stuffed ornate furnishings of the Victorian era might look out of place to the resident of a small, contemporary apartment. The "right" look changes with the passage of time. My sixties beehive hairdo captured in old photos serves me as a reminder of this fact.

Consider feng shui as a viable choice when you are searching for ways to improve your life. At times its applications are right on the mark and are "just what the doctor ordered". At times feng shui cures can be used together with other methodologies. And sometimes feng shui will work differently than you could have ever imagined.

It is most important to understand that a living environment intertwines with life in a significant way. In the words of Sir Winston Churchill:

"We shape our buildings and our buildings shape us."

Feng shui will increase the likelihood that your life will be forever improved.

Chapter Two

History of Feng Shui

Background

Few things express the Chinese culture more exquisitely than feng shui. It is an amalgamation of the pragmatic and the idealistic, of science and spiritualism. It reveres the past even as it uses the present to prepare for the future.

Originating in China approximately 2,000 years ago, feng shui found fertile ground in China's belief systems and inclusive geographical features. By 500 A.D., feng shui had become so integrated into the culture that all people--emperors to peasants--used its guidelines to create their living spaces.

One might then legitimately wonder why it has taken so long for feng shui to be recognized in the West. The answer to this requires some knowledge of China's history. Until the end of World War II, feng shui was practiced by almost everyone in China. Although the imperial system was replaced by the Nationalist government in 1928, it was only after World War II that the country was physically and culturally divided by the Communists when they ousted the Nationalists from the mainland.

On the Chinese mainland, the Communist government launched a bloody campaign to purge feng shui and other "feudal practices" from their culture. To date, they have been successful in abolishing feng shui from the mainstream. If it is practiced at all, it is done discreetly.

On the island of Taiwan, however, a democratic government was put into place by a new generation of Chinese eager to absorb Western culture. Feng shui was not in official disfavor but it was put on the back burner by a population that did not look upon it as an exportable commodity. Many young Chinese spurned the traditional practice in favor of contemporary architecture and design. Only today as the East feels secure in its place in the contemporary world is feng shui gaining widespread recognition.

While feng shui was still practiced by many in both Chinas it lost much of its vitality as local superstitions diluted its philosophical center. Feng shui became simplistic, and its central principles became fixated on few issues.

One such issue involved the selection of a family member's grave. Indeed, to some Chinese, feng shui is simply the art of finding the best location for a burial plot. It is believed that a properly placed grave site will ensure the prosperity of future generations. With such a limited focus, it is understandable why feng shui did not gain worldwide acceptance.

When feng shui was cast out of the mainstream another ingredient necessary to keep feng shui viable and alive was lost--the capacity to incorporate new information. Kept isolated and apart from twentieth century Western communications, information and influences, feng shui seemed arcane and dated.

Even publications in English were frozen in a 19th century point-of-view. Rev. Ernest J. Eitel's 1873 book on feng shui was one of the few written by a Westerner prior to the 1970's. And even during the twentieth century, most books on the subject were written by Sinophiles from their Eastern perspective. Thus, very few feng shui ideas have been filtered through Western ideology.

Karma

Unlike other ancient cultures, the Chinese did not rely on prayer alone to beseech favors of the forces of the Universe. Their religious beliefs stated that one's actions created a destiny in this life or the next.

The word Karma defines this concept. It suggests that life is not an isolated entity but is part of an ongoing process. One's actions are cumulative, adding up like points in a game. The highest goal is the attainment of perfection or total goodness. Should one stray from the path of virtue, one is karmically kicked back by experiencing hardships. Simply put, if you do harm, harm will befall you; if you perform good deeds then good fortune will follow. Feng shui reinforces the concept of karma. It encourages us to examine our interaction with the environment in light of future consequences.

Taoism
(pronounced Dowism)

The Chinese philosophy known as Taoism also contributed to the development of feng shui.

Literally, Taoism means, "the Way" or "the Path". This philosophy states that all things are interconnected and that any alteration, elimination or disregard of any one part must be measured against the effects on all other parts. According to Tao, the whole takes precedence over the individual. (Taoism is discussed in detail in Chapter III)

Karma and Taoism nurture an atmosphere in which one is encouraged to scrutinize one's inner actions, and the notion that the individual is a higher or more important form of life is foreign. These parallel belief systems provided fertile ground for the germination of feng shui.

China's Landscape

China's topography is diverse and dramatic. Soaring mountain ranges, broad expanses of flat lands and twisting rivers create a landscape that demands attention.

The agrarian society of China both revered and feared the forces of nature. Instead of trying to control nature, the Chinese were inclined to observe and find ways to maximize nature's benefits. This approach is illustrated in one feng shui suggestion for an ideal building site. Feng shui suggests that it is best to have a hill or a stand of trees to the north of a home, for they will help to block the cold north winds that descend upon China each winter. A protected home is easier to keep warm. These kinds of feng shui recommendations were practiced long before the West understood the benefits of passive solar concepts.

Geomancers, The Doctors of Feng Shui

Geomancers are feng shui professionals. The name geomancer (diviner of geographic features) didn't become popular until the 18th century although feng shui professionals have practiced for the last two thousand years.

The early practitioners, all male, were a colorful lot. Garbed in long vivid robes, these sages often were carried to a site on a conveyance that resembled a combination gurney and Mardi Gras float. The geomancer's repertoire included a profound understanding of the natural world, a little bit of psychology and a showman's sense of drama.

When a geomancer was hired to help select a building site, the following was one method used. A distinguished gentleman, dressed from head to toe in yellow or red, is carried on a decorated stretcher to the top of a mountain. He alights and instructs his porters to blindfold him. Then, in a grand gesture of fearless determination, he faces the appropriate direction and proceeds to run, pell mell, down the mountain slope until he trips and falls to the ground. His attendants rush to pick him up and place a marker on the g r o u n d where he fell. They carry him to the top again, and, from a slightly different vantage point, he repeats the entire process until there are sufficient markers dotted along the mountain side or he has perhaps sprained his ankle.

Comical though this may seem, it was actually a viable method to use for uncovering hidden geographical features prior to the development of sophisticated equipment. The geomancer was locating depressions or low spots on the ground that could indicate hollow spaces that might represent either a fault underneath the earth's surface, a water aquifer or perhaps a mineral deposit. Each has the capacity to cause damage. The fault might be a vent for volcanic activity, causing a foundation to crack or shift, streams of water underneath a building's foundation might result in moisture problems and mineral deposits might emit a dangerous substance like radon. By using himself in lieu of sophisticated equipment, the geomancer located safe building sites for his clients.

Failure to heed the advice of a geomancer could portend doom. Bad feng shui is given as one of the explanations for the downfall of the Ch'in dynasty (211-207 B.C.). Most of the Great Wall of China was built during the Ch'in dynasty. Designed to provide an impenetrable defense, this gigantic barrier was, according to the geomancers of the time, a razor that cut the life blood from the earth. Thus, instead of shielding the Chinese from harm, the Great Wall acted as a knife that severed the unity of the land. The Ch'in dynasty became weak in the same way that the Great Wall undermined the land by slicing it apart.

In Hong Kong today, geomancers work hand in hand with engineers and architects who design buildings for big businesses. For example, the Hong Kong and Shanghai Bank, which recently announced an annual profit of $1.9 billion, consulted a geomancer before constructing its new 47-story, $670 million headquarters.

The Trump Organization is employing feng shui principles in developing the billion dollar Riverside South project, built to revitalize New York's westside. The project's partner from Hong Kong has helped the Trump Organization recognize the importance of feng shui.

Geomancers are also invited into apartments and houses of individuals to recommend furniture and accessory placement or methods to eliminate bad feng shui. Advice of the modern geomancer is so popular that there is a nightly television program that dispenses guidance to its audience in Hong Kong.

Schools of Feng Shui

There are two traditional schools of feng shui: the Compass School and the Form School. A third school -- the Pyramid School -- is new.

Compass School

The Compass School believes that proper placement is the strongest single element to determine a successful living space. Depending upon date of birth, date of occupancy, or numerology of a name, favorable alignments are determined for each individual.

The Compass School uses a unique compass called a luopan. A luopan can have as many as 36 concentric circles beneath a magnetic arrow. Each circle is devoted to one specific category of information such as the five elements, the 64 I-Ching symbols or the signs of the Chinese Zodiac. Finding the best alignment for a physical location in each category is the task of the geomancer in the Compass School.

Recommendations in the Compass School are based not on hard scientific, social or physical facts but rather on the study of

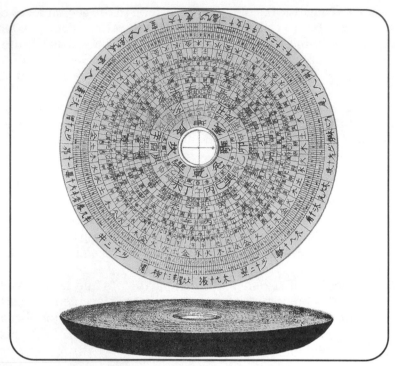

Loupan

sacred geometry which suggests that all parts of reality can be visualized as being connected with lines. The lines should form configurations that match the geometric patterns present in all molecules. Certain combinations of angles occur frequently in these minute particles, and, if the placement of objects in our world can duplicate these combinations, we can become part of the harmony of all things. Harmony enhances the attainability of personal success.

Form School

The Form School bases its suggestions on the observation of the natural world. Structural phenomena like mountain ranges, buildings or waterways are analyzed for their effect on the human condition. Followers search for the influence these shapes and forms have on the quality of life. The geomancer who runs down the hill is a representative of the Form School.

Once a group of businesswomen sought my advice on the purchase of a commercial building. I used the approach that a Form School advocate would to evaluate the situation. I observed the physical location to discover clues to the feng shui quotient in the surrounding area. The building was on a road that meandered next to an unpolluted and free-flowing river. The vegetation in the area was healthy, and the businesses and homes on this road had prospered. The glaring exception was the building under consideration. Abandoned cars parked on the front lawn, a dilapidated exterior and even an eviction notice stapled to the front door were some of the signs of failure.

When I looked further, I saw that a high cement tower across the street was the culprit. The Form School would suggest that, when one structure looms over another, the occupants of the smaller one will suffer misfortune. After observing negative conditions, the Form School geomancer can offer suggestions to mitigate bad feng shui.

In this manner, the Form School considers the natural world and evaluates its physical presence.

Pyramid School

Unlike the Form and Compass schools, the Pyramid School does not single out one methodology. It draws from both traditional schools as well as from other disciplines. The Pyramid School is all-inclusive, using any information system whenever appropriate. History teaches us that inflexible systems often topple and any time that a field of knowledge is considered to be "the absolute truth" it is sure to be undermined. Thus, the Pyramid School includes flexible parameters which allow the addition of new information.

Accepting theories that have either scientific proof or are supported by a belief system, the Pyramid School separates them into two categories, hard fact and soft fact. Hard facts are those that can be proven through current scientific knowledge while soft facts are those ideas we feel are true. The Pyramid School expands feng shui's foundation because it includes new information and creates a niche for the latest discoveries.

It is human to try to understand how things work; and what we don't know, we try to make known. This human trait is often observable in the actions of Alzheimer's victims. My friend's mother will invent stories to cover the lapses in her memory with what she believes should be true. Caretakers of Alzheimer's patients refer to this as "confabulating". In our lives, when we see things that we cannot explain, we invent explanations, much as an Alzheimer's patient does. Some perceived truths are, in fact, no more than a desire to understand. What is true today may topple tomorrow. Ferreting out the truth as it exists at each juncture in time is the work of the Pyramid School which incorporates current knowledge as well as the specific requirements of a culture's point of view. This book derives its reasoning from this approach.

The shards of the past cannot become whole until we cement them with current knowledge.

Writing a New Chapter in Feng Shui's History

Certain experiences are common to all people. In The Power of Myths*, Joseph Campbell made us aware of the universality of legends to all cultures. He points out that the stories may differ slightly in detail, but they all seek to satisfy the same questions.

When a culture does not have the scientific knowledge to answer these questions, the answers are based on generations of experiential wisdom and intuitive extrapolations.

The stories through which a culture teaches its principles and guidelines are alike because human beings share fundamental emotional needs. And myths are the stuff that provide a method of dealing with these needs.

How to create the best possible life for oneself and one's family is the root of all questions, whether it be basic survival or the nuances of actualization.

How to stay healthy.
How to sustain a fulfilling relationship.
How to create a path that will lead to success in life.

These are some of the universal questions for which solutions are sought.

Feng shui is not unique in the sense that it seeks to answer fundamental questions of the human condition. It stands apart because it unites the individual's success with his/her living space. How we inhabit the planet is integral to our experience.

* *The Power of Myths*, Joseph Campbell, 1988

18

Chapter Three

ABC's of Feng Shui

Tao, Yin & Yang and Ch'i

Tao, yin & yang and ch'i are Chinese words for concepts that you may already have thought about and integrated into your life. Only the names may be unfamiliar.

An explanation of these terms will enable you to understand the reasoning behind many of feng shui's teachings.

Taoism
(pronounced Dowism)

Like the ripples created by tossing a stone into a pond of water, our actions change the waters in the sea of humanity. We are linked together in a chain of interdependency.

For centuries, the Chinese have embraced this idea through the philosophy/ religion called Taoism. Translated literally, tao means "the way". It inspires us to find a place for ourselves in a natural process that does not disrupt the function of the whole. Acceptance of our place in the scheme of things deepens our concern for the consequences of our actions.

Science tells us that for every action there is a reaction. Consider the chain of events that lead to rain. The process begins when the sun evaporates the earth's surface waters. Then the water molecules accumulate until they burst forth as rain from saturated clouds. Without knowledge of this cycle, it would appear that sunshine had nothing to do with rain when, in fact, it is essential. We cannot always predict how our actions will affect the world around us, but we can be sure that they will.

Here is an event from my childhood that illustrates the principle of tao.

As a child, I lived in northern New Jersey after World War II. It was a time of great exodus from the crowded cities to suburban areas. The appeal of fresh air, trees and uncrowded conditions enticed many families to move. Automobiles and better highways were essential to stimulate this migration as the wage earner usually continued to work in the city. The rush to provide housing for this burgeoning group fueled the new industry of affordable mass-produced housing. Enter the land developer/ subdivision builder.

One large farm in my town was bought by a local developer. It was subdivided with a single goal in mind--maximum profits. If a hill was in the way, it was leveled. If a stand of old oak trees impeded the heavy equipment's path, they were cut down. Because the vegetation was stripped and the hills were razed, the land's fertile top soil was washed away by rain.

On the banks of a river that meandered through the property, the builder crowded as many homes as possible since river front houses were the highest in price. Unfortunately, these houses were built on a flood plain, and, within a few years, heavy spring rains caused the river to rise over its banks. Homes in its path were flooded, and each family watched their possessions soak up the waters like a blotter sponging up black ink.

Cleaning up eventually became more than each homeowner's individual responsibility. Residents in other parts of my town were taxed for funds to construct a spillway to catch the overflow. Had the developer cared about accommodating nature, this calamity could have been averted.

The destruction of rain forests, extinction of animal and plant species, and emergence of a flawed ozone layer--all these are the result of ignoring tao.

Tao teaches us to be aware of how nature works; it teaches us to accommodate the scheme of things rather than manipulate the natural world to fit human schemes. In the case of the builder/ developer, circumventing tao created a disaster.

There are simple ways to keep in touch with nature in our daily lives. Place a desk near a window, listen to water bubbling in a fish tank, place a plant or fresh flower near a favorite chair, or enjoy feeling a smooth stone in the palm of your hand. All of these allow you to understand that any damage to the natural world ultimately damages you.

Uniting individual parts to form a whole is another way of expressing a connection to the tao. A single faint sound can become a roar when joined by like noises in a chorus.

A home should have a self-contained shape as does our earth. Any room with three walls jutting out from the main outline of the building (see below) is not considered to be as lucky as a room whose perimeter is contained within the building's overall shape. To be enveloped in the heart of a building helps us to absorb its collective energy as it bolsters our feeling of connectedness.

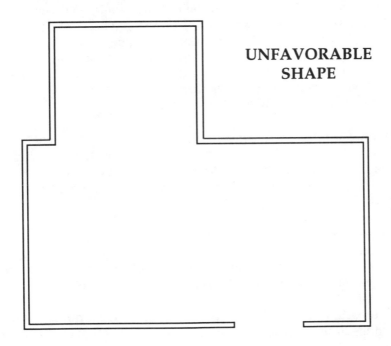

UNFAVORABLE SHAPE

It is imperative that we have connectedness in our lives in order to feel complete within our society. This is evident in the way we have chosen to punish social offenders. They are incarcerated; forced to live without the role of connectedness which is so central to our well-being.

In order to consider Taoist principles, ask these kinds of questions when selecting a building lot, buying a home or arranging furniture:

1. Will the land be disturbed by building on it?
2. Can nature be experienced from within the building?
3. Does the home's floor plan support a sense of unity?

When our planet's needs are considered to be as important as the individual's, all will thrive.

Yin and Yang

Yin and yang express the concept of opposites. Yin is dark, sweet, curved and expansive while yang is light, spicy, straight and contracted. Yet, unlike the Western concept of opposites, the Chinese view yin and yang as mutually supportive.

Consider the expression "All work and no play makes Jack a dull boy." Jack, presumably, would not be dull if he balanced work and play. Although work and play represent the opposite ends of the spectrum, both are essential to produce a balance in Jack's personality. To ensure our health, we should exercise vigorously and get enough rest. To pass fair judgment, we need to listen to both sides. To drive a car safely, we must be alert while relaxed. Optimum conditions are created by balancing opposites.

Combining opposites neutralizes the intense effect of each. A candle doesn't light the entire world at night nor does drawing a curtain completely darken a room during the day. However, introduction of a contrasting element tends to lessen the intensity of the original condition.

For example, the next time you bite into a hot pepper, place some sugar on the spot in your mouth that feels on fire instead of seizing the nearest glass of water. Sugar will dissipate the effect of hot pepper and the spicy (yang) sensation will be mitigated by the sweet (yin).

Yin and yang in combination create balance. Equanimity in our surroundings provides a supportive foundation that allows us to listen to our inner voice.

Adele Davis, the pioneering nutritionist, found that children choose foods that provide all the appropriate nutrients if allowed to select what to eat. Homeostasis (inner stability) is the state we gravitate toward in all areas, and, when not distracted, we instinctively find a way to maintain balance.

There are certain situations where extremes can be used to elicit a specific reaction. For example, an interrogation room lit by one bright light above the head of an accused individual is a staple of old police films. The uncomfortable illumination coerces a criminal into confessing. The volume of illumination in a hospital operating room is too bright for one's living room, but it is essential for the task at hand.

In the absence of extenuating circumstances, feng shui suggests balancing extremes in the following areas:

1.   lighting;
2.   color;
3.   group activity space vs. individual activity space;
4.   walking space vs. sitting space.

A level of peace and contentment can be achieved when we weave variety into the tapestry of our lives. This can be the first step to achieving balance.

Ch'i
(rhymes with "tea")

Ch'i is the Chinese word for energy. Everything is animated by energy. Ch'i is the spark of life, the ignition for our motions and motivations; it is the doer, the achiever, the activator, the energizer. Feng shui teaches that the single most important consideration in any environment is how ch'i is inhibited or enhanced.

Walk into any room filled with people and observe the variety of ch'i exhibited by each individual. Some may be described as vivacious, dynamic, lively, powerful, energetic or vigorous when positive. Others may appear hostile, defensive, aggressive or belligerent when negative. These descriptions provide a listener with a knowledge of the energy (ch'i) expended by that person. Upbeat, positive energy is a magnet that draws us; and it is almost always desirable.

While watching a football game at my son's college, I was struck by the fact that cheerleading is truly "ch'i-leading". A cheerleader's task is to marshal enthusiasm which, in turn, motivates the players. A motivated player is energized into winning a game. Hard work and perseverance are necessary in order to achieve success, and both of these elements require the use of personal energy.

Ch'i flows within all life forms. The veins of the earth through which water and minerals travel are conductors of ch'i in the same way our body's veins and arteries carry blood. Just as ingesting toxic chemicals into our body can harm our health, pollution of aquifers can destroy the earth's well-being. In each case, the ch'i is challenged to survive.

No movement is necessary to express ch'i. Immobile objects exude ch'i. Consider the Rocky Mountains. Their form alone radiates energy. Just as mountains demand attention, certain stationary objects in one's home will stand out.

Vegetation communicates energy by changing its form. The healthy, verdant tree whose leaves create a lush mosaic percolates vitality, whereas the dying leaves in the fall become stiff, drained of color and are no longer as responsive to the movement of the air. We perceive vitality or ch'i through these changes.

Energy should flow unobstructed within a space. We feel the effects of blocked energy every time we have a cold.

Not only must energy be unimpeded, it should be supported by clearly defined passageways. I had a girlfriend who lived in a home built in the style of the architect Frank Lloyd Wright. The front door opened into a huge open space, and the distance between the front door and the first furniture grouping seemed enormous. Intimidating, highly polished marble floors extended in every direction. No matter how many times I visited this house, my discomfort never waned. Even though I didn't know about feng shui, I realized that the lack of clearly defined routes through this space caused my distress. This house violated the feng shui guideline that there must be clear cut and appropriate pathways of ch'i from the entrance to most areas.

Ch'i moves through nature, through our homes, and through ourselves. It is important to find a way to support and encourage appropriate energy in our lives.

The tao, yin and yang and ch'i are the alphabet upon which the language of feng shui builds. When you are equipped with an understanding of feng shui's foundation, you are ready to explore its contents.

Designing Your Happiness

Chapter Four

Test Your Home's Feng Shui Quotient

Health

We do not generally notice the state of our health until we become ill. Yet without our health, very little else can be accomplished.

Nutritious food, exercise and periodic check-ups are accepted ways to maintain physical health. Feng shui adds another dimension to our care. A physical environment can heal or it can cause illness.

When I took my 6'4" teenage son, Zachary, to Spain I noticed him tilt his head at a peculiar angle as he passed from room to room in the medieval houses we toured. The door frames were actually high enough for him, but the proximity of his head to the top of the frame didn't give him the confidence to remain erect as he passed through. I shudder to think of the neck problems he might have developed had we lived in one of those medieval houses. Thus, we can look at our living spaces to determine whether the cause for an ailment lies there.

The following test is designed to help you assess your home's environment in relation to health issues. Know, however, that you can be healthy in an unsupportive environment or sick in an ideal environment. As with all areas of your life, you should try to create the most nurturing surroundings.

Health Quiz

Sketch the outline of your entire home as if you were overhead looking down. Indicate with arrows the orientations of north, south, east and west. Use the direction of the rising sun as east. If you live in an apartment, use the shape of your unit only.

Some questions have more than one answer. Record all positive and negative scores. If you cannot answer a question, record a zero and move on to the next.

1.   Can you see any vegetation outside the windows of your kitchen or main gathering rooms?

> +2 if yes in both rooms
> +1 if yes in one room
> -1 if no in one room
> -2 if no in both rooms

2.   Does your entrance foyer have natural light, a view to another room or live plants?

> +1 for view
> +1 for plants
> +1 for light
> -1 for each no

3.   Is there a desk or sitting area at the end of a long hallway?

> -2 for yes

4.   Is there any stagnant water within view of your home year round or seasonally?

> -2 if yes year round
> -1 if yes seasonally

5.   Are any shades of green or yellow part of the decor in your kitchen, living room, family room or bedroom?

> +1 per room if yes

6. Do any faucets in your home leak or drip?

    -2 per leak if yes

7. Are there exposed ceiling beams above your dining table or stove?

    -1 for each beam

8. Is there an exposed ceiling beam, rafter or soffit over your bed?

    -2 for yes

9. Are there exposed rafters or beams above any other sitting areas in your house?

    +2 if no per area
    -2 if yes per area

10. Do you keep live plants or fresh flowers near your bed?

    +1 if yes

11. When in bed can you see your bedroom door without having to look over your shoulder (i.e. turn your head more than 45 degrees?)

    +2 if you don't have to turn your head
    -2 if you have to turn it more than 45 degrees

12. Is your reflection in a mirror the first thing you see each morning immediately after getting out of bed?

    -2 if yes

13. Does the ceiling slope over your bed?

    -1 if yes

14. Does the head of your bed back up against a wall?

> +2 if yes
> -1 if no

15. Does the door of your bedroom open so that the door is flat against an adjacent wall?

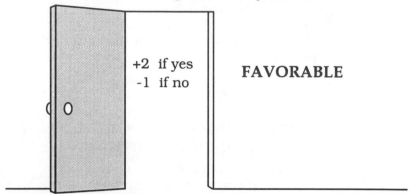

> +2 if yes
> -1 if no

FAVORABLE

16. Is your bedroom over an empty but enclosed space (like a crawl space)?

> -2 if yes

17. Do you have a bathroom wall common with a kitchen wall or a bedroom wall?

> -2 if yes

18. Do any of your toilets fail to flush completely or back up frequently?

> -2 if yes per toilet

19. Does your front door have the same proportion to the facade of your home as a mouth does to a face?

> +2 if approximately the same proportion
> -1 if smaller than a mouth is to a face
> -1 if larger than a mouth is to a face

20. Is your favorite place to sit in your living room facing the room's entrance door?

+1 if yes

How to Score the Health Quiz

Total all positive and negative scores to arrive at one positive or negative number.

Analysis of Scoring
Explanations for the test questions are found in the chapters dealing with each room or area being considered.

+14 to +21   You have the potential to be the picture of health.

+1 to +13   Your environment supports efforts to stay healthy; minor adjustments will allow you to stay fit with less effort.

0 to -12   Achieving optimum health will be easier if you make adjustments in your home.

-13 to -24   Your surroundings are of no support in maintaining your health. Make some changes immediately.

Relationships

Whether it's your home or workplace, there is usually some space that you share with other human beings. Imagine how different your childhood might have been had you lived in the same house with a larger or smaller family. The arrangement of our interior spaces can influence the quality of our interactions.

Consider the seating arrangement at a traditional dining room table. It is not by chance that father and mother typically sit at opposite ends of a rectangular table. These positions offer a vantage point consistent with the role of a parent or guardian.

1.   There is a direct line of vision to the other diners.

2.   There is more freedom of movement than for those who sit next to others.

3.   More often than not, the narrower part of a table commands a view of the room's entrance.

Some families have discarded this seating arrangement because the power of the family is no longer as centralized in the parents. Today a more egalitarian structure often exists.

Goals of relationships are more often actualized when mutual. Implicit in all feng shui remedies is the aim that the results will benefit all parties. This test can help alert you to those areas in your home that may be influencing relationships.

Relationship Quiz

Follow the same set of instructions as in the Health Quiz.

1.   Are there any doors in your home that are not opened at least once a week? (do not include closet or attic doors.)

        +2 if all interior & exterior doors are used
        -2 for each unused door inside the home
        -1 for each unused door leading out-of-doors

2.   In what direction does the most frequently used entrance door to your home face?

        +2 if south, east or southeast
        -1 if west
        -2 if north

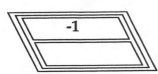

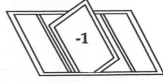

3.   Do the majority of windows in your
home swing from hinges or crank
horizontally at a 45 degree angle
so that they can be totally opened?
Or are the majority double hung?

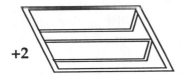

+2 if majority open at least
45 degrees
-2 if majority don't open at all
-1 if majority open partially

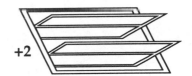

4.   Are there at least three windows for each
door or entryway into your living room,
family room or kitchen?

+1 for each room with exactly 3 windows
per entryway or door
-1 for each room with more than 3 windows per entryway or door
-1 for each room with less than 3 windows
per entryway or door

5.   On which side of the house (north, south, east or
west) is your main gathering room (either living
room or family room)?

+2 if south
+1 if east or southeast
-2 if west or north

6.   What is the shape of your dining table?

+2 if round or octagonal
-1 if rectangular
+1 if square or oval and the length is less than double the width
-1 if rectangular or oval and length is more than double the width

7.   How many chairs are placed at your dining table?

+1 if the number is even
-1 if the number is odd

8.   Are the edges on your bed's headboard mostly rounded?

+2 if mostly rounded corners
-2 if corners are right angles or sharp
-1 if you have no headboard

9.   What room is in the geographical center of your home?

+2 if it is the main gathering room
+1 if it is the kitchen
-2 if it is a bathroom
-2 if it is a hallway

10.   The physical location of your bedroom in your home is important. What, if any, applies to yours?

+2 near other bedrooms but separated by a closet or bathroom
-2 three of the walls are common with the outside
-2 if a toilet is next to a wall that separates the bathroom from the bedroom (if there is a closet on that wall, it is not considered a common wall.)

Answer the following questions if you are married or have a live-in relationship.

11. Do you and your partner

>   +2 share the same closet
>   +1 have adjacent closets
>   -2 have your closets in different rooms

12. Is your favorite place to be in your home

>   +2 the same room as your partner's favorite place?
>   -1 in a different room from your partner's favorite place?

13. What describes your sleeping arrangements?

>   +2 one mattress
>   -1 two mattresses pushed together
>   -2 two separate beds

Total all positive and negative scores to arrive at one positive or negative number.

Analysis of Scoring

Explanations for the test questions are located in the chapters dealing with room or area being considered.

If you answered only the first ten questions:

+9 to +18   Your home fosters excellent relationships.

+1 to +8   Your relationships are generally supported by your environment. With minor adjustments, good ones can become great.

0 to -13   Your living space is hindering good relationships. Change some conditions to promote positive changes.

-14 to -26   It may be extremely difficult to cultivate good relationships in this atmosphere. Make changes as soon as possible.

If you answered all thirteen questions:

+12 to +21   Your environment supports excellent relationships.

+1 to +13   For the most part, your home is not hindering
your involvement with others. With a few adjustments, conditions can be optimum.

0 to -15   The status quo is not contributing favorably to
relationships. Make changes in your home.

-16 to -32   It may be extremely difficult to maintain good
relationships in this atmosphere. Alter your
environment as soon as possible.

Self Actualization
(Financial Success)

A feeling of personal worth comes from activities that utilize our talents and elevate our self-esteem. Walking down a path that is illuminated by our own desires is one of life's joys. When we are involved in an activity that makes us happy we are likely to feel satisfied with our level of success. Thus, success means far more than making money. Many times, however, the two go hand in hand. Tapping into our own personal potential makes life sunny.

Traditionally, the third area which feng shui addresses is labeled financial success. I have broadened this concept to include the idea of self-actualization.

Consider how shifting one piece of furniture can help reverse an unsatisfactory situation.

A friend's daughter was having difficulty concentrating on her homework. She had no problem focusing on work at school, yet at home she was easily distracted.

Searching for a feng shui explanation, I discovered two things. Her desk was positioned perpendicular to a window on the west side of the house and her right shoulder faced the window when she was seated.

This arrangement broke two feng shui rules.

1. A place of contemplation or study should not be on the west side of a house.

2. One's writing arm should never be on the same side as the source of light.

Consider why these two rules make sense.

Sitting at a desk facing the afternoon sun does not contribute to optimum performance because to try to study or concentrate in the glare of the setting sun is a distraction and, indeed, an outright hardship.

The writing arm must not obstruct the source of light. This young lady sat facing south with her right arm closest to the window. Since she was right-handed, the sunlight shining over her right shoulder created shadows on the work area. These shadows that danced with the rhythm of her arm movement interfered with her concentration.

The solution I proposed was that the desk be moved to another location in the room and that the chair be positioned so that her writing arm would not interfere with the light source.

This concept may be applied to all situations no matter what the light source might be--a table lamp, a floor light, or an overhead light. Avoid obstructing the source of light; this may hamper your pursuit of excellence.

Take this test to determine your feng shui self-actualization quotient.

Self-Actualization Quiz
(Financial Success)

Draw an outline of your home and follow the directions in the Health Quiz.

    1.   In what direction does the most frequently used entrance door to your home face?

               +2 if southeast
               +1 if directly south or east
               -2 if north or northwest
               -1 if west

    2.   What is the shape of the path (inside or outside) that leads to your home's entrance door? (the route you select, whether predetermined or not, is the path).

               +2 if undulating with curves
               +1 if crescent shaped
               -1 if straight
               -2 if it turns at a 90 degree angle

3. When you walk through the front door of your home you see

    +2 a fish tank
    -1 another door leading outside
    -1 a parallel solid wall within ten feet
    -2 a stairway directly in front of the door

4. Can you see any water source (pond, pool, lake, river, stream, or ocean) near your property? If you do, what direction do you face while viewing it?

    +2 southeast
    +1 south or east
    -1 north

5. Is this water source

    +2 gently moving and clean
    +1 seasonal
    -2 rapidly flowing
    -2 non-existent
    -2 stagnant or polluted

6. Is a wall of any bathroom common with

    -2 the kitchen
    -2 the front door
    -1 your bedroom
    -1 your study room

7. During most of the year is your front door

    +2 at the end of a path that is widest where it meets the street?
    +1 visible from the street or where you park?
    -1 hidden from view even partially by trees or shrubs?

8. Are any shades of red used in and around your home?

    +2 in a main gathering room
    +1 in an auxiliary gathering room, study or kitchen
    +1 if any house or garden plants are red
    +1 if red or its related colors are part of your wardrobe

9. Is the exterior shape of your home

    +2 U-shaped?
    +1 an octagon?
    +1 square or rectangle?
    -2 L-shaped?
    -1 For any room that protrudes like a peninsula from the main shape of the house

10. Does your front door have the same proportions to the facade of your home as a mouth does to a face?

    -2 if much smaller
    +1 if the proportions are close to those of a mouth to a face

11. Do any toilets continue to run after they are flushed?

    -2 if yes

12. Do you have a separate room in which to pursue your interests, hobbies or work?

    +2 if you have an entire room
    +1 if you have a designated private space, like a desk, drawing table, etc. as part of a room
    -1 if you don't have a permanent place and have to work on a make-shift space, like a kitchen table, a bed, etc.

13.   Do you have a beam or a slanted ceiling over your hobby or work area?

        -2 if yes

Analysis of Scoring
Explanations for the test questions are located in the chapters dealing with the room or area being considered.

+14 to +25	You have a supportive environment which nurtures your life's dreams.
+1 to +13	Achieving your life's goals may be easier with minor adjustments.
0 to -10	Your efforts are sapped by your environment. Adjustments in your cnvironmcnt will hclp you bc morc productive.
-11 to -20	Your efforts could be sabotaged by your living space. Remove these obstacles from your environment.

It would now be helpful to make a list of specific problems that might be eliminated by using feng shui remedies. Keep this list handy to help you locate the cures for your specific situations.

A list might look like this:

1.   Why do I often wake up with sore muscles in my shoulders?
2.   Why do I fight with my spouse at the breakfast table?
3.   What can I do about my teenager's rebellious attitude?
4.   How can I feel less anxious when I'm home alone?
5.   How can my hobby become my livelihood?

Armed with new knowledge of how your home is impacting your health, your relationships and your self-actualization, you are ready to discover how feng shui can transform negative surroundings into positive ones.

Chapter Five

Essential Components of Feng Shui

Water, Light, Vegetation...

To create a successful home setting it is vital to understand the feng shui view of water, light, direction, topography, vegetation, shape, architectural details and color. While feng shui provides us with very specific applications for these elements, you can, many times, rely on your own intuition to guide you, as long as it is not obscured by convention or habit.

Water

Water is the most important element in feng shui. Evaluating its location, currents and purity is paramount to producing optimum health, happiness and success. Water near or inside a dwelling can assist in channeling good fortune to your life. Feng shui teaches that viewing water brings good luck. However, if you don't happen to live next to a body of clear moving water, there are acceptable alternatives. Know that you can secure the benefits of viewing water by choosing to place a bird bath in your yard or a small fish tank in your house. How many Chinese restaurants have you visited that have fish tanks? These aquariums are a feng shui talisman to insure business success.

The wish to be close to water seems universal, based upon a comparison of the costs of property with and without water views. Water is essential to the well-being of our bodies both inside and outside. Since our bodies are composed mostly of water, it seems reasonable to assume that clean water brings luck and tainted water portends disaster.

Water can adjust our mental attitude by altering our ch'i. We can feel exhilarated by breathing the ocean air or soothed by a woodland lake. The negatively charged ions or the minerals sprayed in ocean mist may contribute to a positive feeling. Whether the water is in the form of an ocean, river, lake, pool or pond, being near water adds quality to our lives. In proximity to clean, flowing waters, we may feel exhilarated or calm; in some way our ch'i will be affected.

Rational explanations will not alter our intrinsic connection to water. We need it to survive physically; we value its presence aesthetically; and we are connected to it in a way that requires no scientific explanation.

If your home has a view of clean, gently flowing water, you are in an ideal feng shui position. The following list reveals optimum conditions as well as those which must be remedied.

Water Outside the Home

Lucky	**Unlucky**
Clean and pristine	Polluted
Moderately flowing	Stagnant
To the east or south	Rapidly flowing

Clean and Pristine vs. Polluted

We all live near water. Even though a home may not be close to a lake, stream or ocean, water is pumped or carried inside for a host of reasons. We drink water, cook with water, and use water to assist us with personal hygiene. Contaminated water is a health risk even if we do not consume it directly. A stagnant pond or puddle caused by improper drainage can be breeding grounds for disease and, hence, harbingers of ill health and bad fortune. There may not be a direct pipeline from a polluted body of water into a home, but tainted waters nearby will ultimately affect us unfavorably.

Severe damage sustained by New York homes adjacent to the contaminated waters of Love Canal, Niagara Falls, is just one of many dramatic examples in our recent history that reflect the enormity of this problem. For years, companies unloaded toxic by-products into the waters of Love Canal. Their actions went unchecked until the people living nearby began to exhibit severe and unusual health problems. The population suffered more birth defects, more cancer and more breathing anomalies than the statistical norm.

Although one person usually cannot clean up an entire body of water, the actions of each of us can ultimately lead to reversing a negative situation. Using pure non-polluting products and donating time, expertise or money to environmental watchdog organizations are steps in the chain of events that lead to change. Every revolution begins with a single voice and every evolution begins with a single action. While using our energy to change the negative status quo, we can deflect the harmful effects of polluted waters by employing feng shui cures.

Just as tainted waters can have a harmful effect, clean moving water can have a salubrious effect. Drinking pure water can detoxify the body. Enjoying the sight of a meandering stream can soothe the spirit. Hearing the bubbling waters of a fountain or fish tank or luxuriating in a tub of hot water can contribute to contentment and relaxation.

Moderately Flowing vs. Stagnant or Rapidly Flowing

The flow rate of water indicates a variety of conditions in the surrounding area. Rapidly flowing rivers and streams are the result of water passing over an underlying fault. These faults might be conduits for volcanic activity or they could house harmful mineral deposits. Sometimes these conditions can be destructive.

Stagnant water is as undesirable as rapidly flowing water. It may be a breeding ground for disease, the source of unpleasant odors or simply be unsightly.

Moderately flowing waters, however, indicate the presence of a uniform sediment, and it is a situation that lacks the dangers described above.

Feng shui suggests that there are symbolic as well as physical dangers inherent in either rapidly flowing or stagnant water. Those who live near rapidly moving rivers or streams may not be able to hold onto money, for money will pass through their lives as quickly as the water that rushes by a river's bank. On the other hand, stagnant water symbolizes the inability to generate income, and efforts to make money are absorbed and evaporated like the water in a puddle.

To gauge the rate of movement that is appropriate for a body of water, consider its size, volume and slope. The normal force of ocean tides are modest when compared to its vast area, but an ocean's rate of flow would be overwhelming for a small lake.

Direction of Water

The best direction from which to view water is the quarter of the pie facing south to east. This direction receives more direct sunlight than others and a sunlit water view is preferable. It inspires and cheers us even as it evinces a healthier environment for its own flora and fauna.

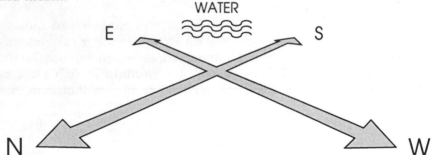

Water Inside the Home

Lucky	**Unlucky**
A fish tank	Bathroom pipes in walls contiguous to dining areas, gathering rooms and bedrooms
Aerating water	Leaks from taps or pipes
	Improperly flushing toilets
	Water next to a fire element

Bathroom Plumbing

At a recent Thanksgiving dinner at my neighbor's home I was able to see why bathroom plumbing in the walls next to a dining area could be unlucky.

I sat next to a guest who, midway through her meal, asked where the bathroom was. I pointed to a door in full view of the dining area, and she seemed mortified.

She started up out of her chair and then changed her mind and sat down again. This happened a couple more times within the next few minutes until she finally excused herself abruptly and rushed out the front door!

Later I learned that she had returned to her sister's house to use the bathroom because she was too embarrassed to be seen entering the bathroom in the host's home. Had she not been able to exercise this option, her digestive process may have become upset. And certainly, had this been her daily environment, she may have developed chronic digestive problems.

Leaking Faucets and Running Toilets

The care given to objects around us often parallels the care we give ourselves. Poorly maintained plumbing often mirrors poor personal maintenance. According to feng shui, leaking faucets and running toilets are harbingers of runny noses and stomach aches. The attention one gives to maintaining the inner workings of a home often mirrors the care one gives to his or her own body. Moreover, those willing to waste water by not repairing these problems are also likely to be wasteful in other ways--they may not be able to hold on to money or may otherwise waste their resources.

Water/ Fire Elements

Fire next to water is inauspicious because water puts out fire and fire can evaporate water. Because these elements can extinguish one another, it is best to keep some distance between the two. Putting a freezer next to a stove impacts both negatively.

The five elements of metal, wood, water, fire and earth should be present in our living spaces. In nature their interdependence is obvious. Wood cannot grow without earth and water, fire cannot burn without wood, metal cannot be formed without earth and earth is replenished by wood. In our homes their presence should mirror the optimum conditions of nature. The harmonious order of the world is disturbed when we place potential adversaries next to each other.

Fish Tanks and Aerating Waters

Water connects us to our genesis and, in that association, we respond to its power.

All too often the water element in a home is relegated to bathrooms and kitchens. The rooms where we gather to socialize, work and rest should feature some representation of this life-sustaining element. Our cup cannot runneth over unless it is first filled.

Light

Just as a lightening bolt transmits energy from the heavens above, light connects us to a source of energy and charges our ch'i. Energy derived from light can motivate and empower us.

Light is a magnet which draws our attention. Neon signs, lighted paths, even near death experiences which are said to begin with an intense change of light--all reflect our attraction to light. Like being in the presence of a charismatic person, light animates those who face it.

According to feng shui, hollow poles lodged in the earth conduct the earth's internal energy to the surface. The area surrounding the apex of a hollow pole will receive the benefits of this energy. These hollow poles like street lights, can be used to define our territory, attract attention and release energy. This force is not unlike the power experienced in the presence of a green canopy of leaves held aloft by a majestic oak.

Light Outside the Home

Lucky	Unlucky
Well-lit pathways	Light that shines in the eyes
Filling out irregular shapes	Dimly lit passageways
Defining boundaries	

Well-lit Pathways

Not only are we attracted to light; our paths are symbolically and actually lit by its presence. Well-lit paths highlight an approach to a home, define its boundaries and provide us with a sense of security.

Filling Out Irregular Shapes

**UNFAVORABLE
SHAPE**

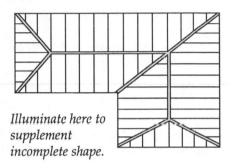

Illuminate here to supplement incomplete shape.

Incomplete shapes, according to feng shui, produce the same results as unfinished tasks. A missing wedge of apple pie or a part of a home with an absent corner suggests the same thing: something has been removed from a complete shape. If a home has a missing section, feng shui suggests that the occupants' best interests may be thwarted.

Unfinished circles, octagons, hexagons, squares or rectangles are considered unlucky. Light can be positioned on the perimeter of the missing segment to supplement the incomplete shape.

**UNFAVORABLE
SHAPE**

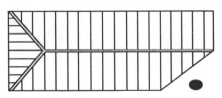

Illuminate here to supplement incomplete shape.

Light Inside the Home

Lucky	**Unlucky**
Brightly lit activity areas	Light that shines in the eyes
Filling out irregular shapes	Dimly lit activity areas
Channeling energy	
Encouraging movement to a room's focus area	
Well-lit passageways	

In addition to the guidelines mentioned for outdoor lighting, indoor lighting also requires other considerations.

Brightly Lit Activity Areas

Provide sufficient light in activity areas. For example, if you want to encourage family members to take off soiled footwear prior to entering the house, illuminate the designated area.

Legitimize relaxing, painting, reading, playing the piano or talking on the telephone by providing enough illumination to encourage these activities.

Change a negative attitude by altering the lighting. If you don't enjoy cooking, try using higher wattage bulbs in the existing kitchen lights or try adding more lighting fixtures. This will brighten your attitude and the area. If your teenager doesn't close his dresser drawers; if males forget to lower toilet seats; if you hate to balance your checkbook, highlight the problem areas with direct lighting and observe the changes that occur.

Filling Out Irregular Shapes

Use light to balance an unbalanced grouping such as a room with an absent corner. (See following page.)

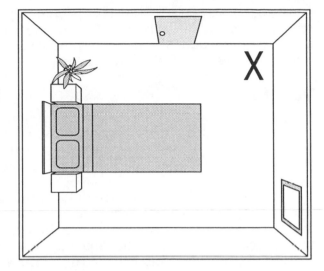

**UNFAVORABLE
(absent corner)**

*Position light in the
area marked "X" to
fill an otherwise
empty, unused corner .*

Channeling Energy

Use light to activate, motivate and energize. It is easier to be propelled into action in the presence of light. Highlighting appropriate areas in our home aids in achieving our life's goals.

Well-lit Passageways

Provide adequate lighting in hallways, stairways and passageways from room to room. Well-defined pathways within a home encourage use of all of its rooms.

Encouraging Movement

Use light to stimulate movement toward the heart of a room. The centered fixture over a dining room table is an appropriate use of light to attract us toward a room's focal point. Be sure to highlight the room's primary use area with a bright light.

Light that Shines in the Eyes

Light must surround and not confront. Light shining directly in the eyes is annoying and unnerving. Lamps in sitting areas should be low so they don't shine in one's eyes when approaching. Any light angled such that it catches the corner of the eye is irritating and not good feng shui.

The Biblical proverb "Don't hide your light under a bushel," reminds us not to conceal our "light"--in other words, our talents and abilities. Do not underestimate the value of light; it assists vision and vision consists of more than what is seen.

Vegetation

Nothing escapes change. Vegetation's seasonal changes unfold before our eyes, but we sometimes don't notice our own physical changes until we happen upon an old photograph.

A plant's condition can offer visual clues to our inner state. Starved, uncared-for vegetation suggests either neglect or misfortune. A wilting bush in the yard can be due to a drought or mismanagement. We care for a plant often in the same way that we care for ourselves; hence the state of our plants can prod us into an awareness of the state of our lives. Taoist philosophy states that our treatment of the immediate world is reflected everywhere.

Learning how to keep plants healthy and devoting time to them mirrors a person's concern for him or herself and the world in general.

Choosing to omit plants from our lives suggests an estrangement from nature. This omission may not produce disaster, but it can contribute to a general feeling of dissatisfaction.

Vegetation exudes ch'i. We must be aware of this on a very primal level. Otherwise, why would we bring flowers to a friend in the hospital? Beautiful blossoms can encourage the life force to triumph over illness. Like clean water in a fish tank, a healthy plant helps create a healthy person. Life begets life.

The age of a plant is another feng shui consideration. Healthy ancient trees, like vibrant venerable sages, are revered in China. Even when it doesn't make economic sense, roadways are often routed around old trees. Cutting down an ancient tree without replacing it by planting others elsewhere is an ominous action that invites disaster.

Including plants in a home reminds one of the partnership that exists between human beings and the natural world. Connecting with the physical world is a high priority in feng shui.

Vegetation Inside Your Home

Lucky	**Unlucky**
Healthy, well-cared for plants	Dying plants
Placed to disguise sharp corners of walls or furniture	No plants
Placed near important activity areas	

Healthy vs. Dying Plants or No Plants

Just as television links us to the commercial world, plants connect us to the natural one. Caring for living things promotes a feeling of well-being and makes us feel useful. Choosing to live without plants produces a dissatisfaction that is not always easy to identify. While not necessarily disastrous, one might experience a general sense of separation from the outside world.

My friends who have homes in both Maine and Florida asked whether it was unlucky not to have plants in the Florida home even though the home in Maine is filled with them. They pointed out that the Florida home had many windows that looked out on vistas of outdoor foliage; hence they didn't need plants inside. According to feng shui, as long as there is a deeply felt connection with vegetation, the positive aspects of living with plants can be satisfied.

Healthy plants reflect our physical, emotional and spiritual care for ourselves.

Hiding Hard Edges

Plants can be utilized in homes where young children play to buffer sharp corners of low glass tables to prevent injury. Everyone should be able to navigate living areas without risk. Any environment should allow free-wheeling movement.

Plants can protect us from the dangers of sharp edges. Through positioning, they can physically prevent us from bumping into obstacles and they can also transform extreme angles into organic shapes.

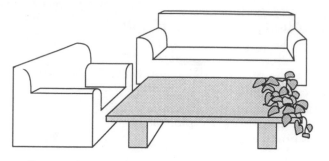

**FAVORABLE
VEGETATION
PLACEMENT**

Protruding wall sections that hide plumbing pipes or heat and cooling ducts should be camouflaged. These ducts or pipes can carry ch'i away from an area, and they can also be conduits for unclean water or air. Using plants to conceal these areas takes advantage of the plants' ch'i which then weakens the effect of hidden negative ch'i.

**FAVORABLE
VEGETATION
PLACEMENT**

Plants Near Important Activity Areas

"She is a breath of fresh air" is an expression used to describe a person's positive impact on a situation. Oxygen, a by-product of green plants, can literally be our breath of fresh air. By placing plants or flowers near important activity areas, we can add to our performance and enjoyment, or alter our perception of a living space.

Including plant life inside a dwelling can increase the energy level (ch'i) therein. Living things exude energy which contributes to our own. It would be easier to live alone on a deserted island than in solitary confinement in a prison. Living alone with nature is easier than living without any connection to the natural world.

Vegetation Outside a Home

Lucky	**Unlucky**
Healthy plant life	Diseased or dying plant life
Planting additional vegetation	Cutting down old or healthy trees
A stand of trees to the north	Vegetation blocking an eastern or southern view

Clearing or Planting

Removing vegetation when building a home is unavoidable. Trees and other shrubbery may need to be cut down to make space for a dwelling. However, land clearing often becomes land obliterating. Vegetation that stands in the way of easy access to the building site is demolished together with the vegetation on the building site. The extra time it takes to circumvent an old tree is viewed as being too much trouble or too expensive. According to feng shui, the removal of a tree requires the planting of one or more trees equal to the one being removed either in age or beauty.

When designing an addition to my home, I had to place it in a space that was occupied by a large old oak tree. The size of my parcel of land and the amount of my available funds were too small to allow me to transplant this granddaddy of oaks. The appropriate feng shui compensation for felling this tree was to plant a few smaller exotic ones elsewhere on my property. I choose two unusual smaller trees as substitutes for the old oak.

A Stand of Trees to the North

The prevailing winds we experience come from the north. Having a barrier protecting the north side of our homes is desirable because it reduces the winds' intensity. The trees can lessen the effects of driving rain and snow or uncomfortably hot or cold breezes.

Symbolically, a stand of trees, a distant mountain range, or a strategically placed boulder lends support to our lives, especially when it is positioned to the north of our homes. The natural predisposition of all animals is to feel safest when its back is protected. Feng shui supports both concepts, ruling that is lucky to have a stand of trees to the north if the north is at the rear of a home.

The Shape of Things

Whether produced by human hands or created by natural forces, the shapes around you mold your life. Just as those who live in the walled valleys of West Virginia are inclined to feel overwhelmed by life, those who live in view of a range of majestic mountains are often inspired with a sense of awe, wonder and adventure.

From mountain ranges to roadways, feng shui urges us to pay attention to the shape of all things.

Feng shui considers straight lines to be suspect at best and harmful at worst. Few things in nature either look or are, in fact, straight. Even towering upright pines give only the appearance of being perfectly upright, for we can usually perceive some tilting as they rise toward the heavens. Only humans try to build with straight lines.

The circle seems to be nature's shape of choice for some of its most dynamic forms. Life as we know it is contained in a circle, and the DNA helix is but a circular spiral.

The circle is merely a curved line whose every point is equidistant from the center. There is no favored position in a circle; no point that is more advantageous. When creating shapes, whether for an entire building or for a furniture arrangement, feng shui advises us to approximate, as much as possible, the spirit of the circle.

It is not accidental that we use the expression "the shape we're in" when we refer to our general well-being. There is a realization at a deep level that shape is critical to a sense of contentment.

Shapes Outside the Home

Lucky	Unlucky
Gently curving paths or roads	Straight paths or roads
Rounded edges	T-Junctures
Contained shapes like circles	Buildings that loom over yours
	Incomplete shapes

Straight Paths vs. Curved Paths

Roadways and paths help us to set our internal speedometer. Life in the proverbial fast lane leads to burn-out. A super highway filled with speeding cars is far less relaxing than a meandering country road. Nerves are often frayed by sitting in traffic, waiting to move. There is usually an appropriate travel speed in any given case.

Any time we go from one situation to another, we need time to change hats. The executive who might bark orders all day long comes home and needs to transition into the role of gentle parent or partner. A curved pathway reduces the pace by increasing the time required to adapt to a new situation. Trees, flowers or other decorations that surround a path can aid in slowing our pace.

The T-Juncture

A house situated directly at the end of a road or a T-juncture, according to the tenets of feng shui, will suffer misfortune. Approaching traffic would seem to be heading directly into the house just as an arrow would pierce a target, and this situation may produce subconscious stress.

However, feng shui points out tendencies and not absolutes, and I am sure that there are many people living in houses located at T-junctures whose lives are just fine. Keep in mind though that just as

UNFAVORABLE HOME LOCATION

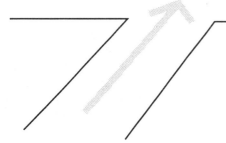

it is easier to stay healthy when one is not exposed to deadly viruses and bacteria, it is better to live in a house not located at a potentially stressful T-juncture.

A Building that Looms Over Yours

If a building larger than yours is situated nearby, you may suffer the effects of "sha ch'i", negative energy.

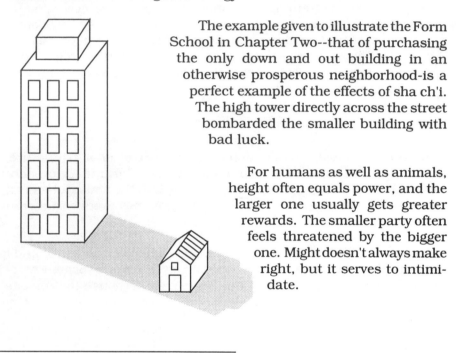

The example given to illustrate the Form School in Chapter Two--that of purchasing the only down and out building in an otherwise prosperous neighborhood-is a perfect example of the effects of sha ch'i. The high tower directly across the street bombarded the smaller building with bad luck.

For humans as well as animals, height often equals power, and the larger one usually gets greater rewards. The smaller party often feels threatened by the bigger one. Might doesn't always make right, but it serves to intimidate.

Incomplete Shapes

A house with a room that protrudes from the main shape is unlucky, because the room that is outside the linear unity of a shape is the proverbial fifth wheel.

Before I was married I experienced the bad luck that accompanies a bedroom which protrudes from the rest of the house. According to feng shui, this room's position outside the heart of the house would keep me from achieving any heartfelt desires. I wanted my master bedroom to be a place I could share with my lifelong partner, but I found that potential partners passed through my life as quickly as a person going through a revolving door. Only after I changed the location of my bedroom to a spot closer to the heart of the house did the door stop spinning. The man who would become my husband then walked into my life and stayed.

Shapes Inside a Home

Lucky	**Unlucky**
Layouts approaching symmetry	Incomplete configurations or prominent asymmetry
Clearly defined pathways	Partially hidden spaces

Symmetrical or Asymmetrical

Symmetry suggests balance and a lack of tension. As an artist, I know that asymmetry creates energy and is far more forceful than symmetry. However, a home should emanate peace. Thus, we are more likely to feel better if furniture arrangements in our homes appear balanced.

Moreover, asymmetrical furniture arrangements can be inconvenient. Communicating with a person sitting on the opposite end of an L-shaped sofa is awkward. The occupants of the two corners have to strain to hear one another. These positions definitely do not encourage intimacy.

Even the shape of our furniture conveys a message. Office furniture consists, more often than not, of unrelieved straight lines. Uninterrupted lines like those of straight back chairs encourage us to stay sharp, keen and attentive. Even during the Renaissance, when furniture was made up of ornate, curved lines, that of the monk's consisted of simple, straightforward shapes. Straight lines imply seriousness of purpose.

Consider yin and yang in relation to shapes. Straight lines are yang or masculine; curved lines are yin or feminine. The following guidelines are useful.

Yang (or Straight) Lines	Yin (or Curved) Lines
Message boards or blackboards	Headboards (rounded edges)
Desks and work stations	Dining tables (octagons, circles or ovals)
Organizational units/ Shelving	Furniture for conversational seating

Feng shui does not endorse any particular style of furniture. Personal selections are the result of one's upbringing. It is important that a line's intrinsic message supports your intentions.

Partially Hidden Spaces

Just as an iceberg presents hidden dangers to ocean voyagers, so do unseen spaces behind doors, underneath floors, and in attics present danger. There often lurks a sense of unease when visible access is denied to parts of a living space.

Crawl spaces under a bedroom or living room are singled out as being particularly harmful. The Chinese believe that such spaces harbor unkind spirits, and, to my mind, these spirits can take the form of rodents, insects or wood rot which can make partially hidden spaces potentially harmful.

Clear Cut Paths

All paths should take us to our destination conveniently, but we often see pathways from a sidewalk to a door that seem untraveled. Instead, well-worn grass paths criss-cross the adjacent lawn; obviously these unused routes are not those with convenient access.

Consider the feng shui belief that it is unlucky to have a stairway facing the entrance door inside a home. If a stairway leads away from the main areas up to the bedrooms, then those returning home might escape to their private space rather than joining other family members in a common room. Stairways in this location will promote the separation of the family, since each person, when walking through the front door, will be drawn to his or her private space. (See next page.)

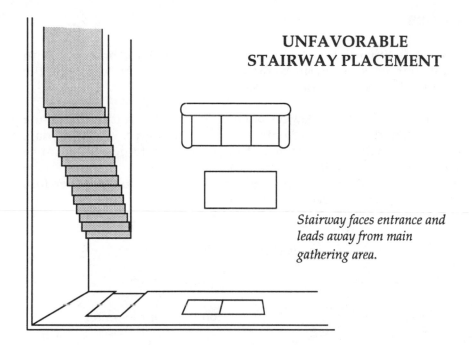

UNFAVORABLE
STAIRWAY PLACEMENT

Stairway faces entrance and leads away from main gathering area.

The layout of a split level home in which one must climb a flight of stairs to arrive at a family's main gathering room can threaten a family's cohesiveness. The difficulty of the approach can be an obstacle to achieving family unity.

A room has to have a clear-cut space to and through it. Major paths, like highways, should lead to common areas. Minor paths, like country roads, can carry us to less traveled places.

Shapes can inspire awe, alienate, and restrict or encourage movement. When selecting furniture, establishing passageways or arranging seating groups, always keep in mind the implicit message that is conveyed by the overall shape.

Architectural Details

Dressing our bodies can be compared to adorning our buildings. Both provide cover even as they reflect a culture's mores, tastes and physical location. The architectural details of our living spaces influence our lives, and both the placement and decorative treatment of doors, windows, ceilings, beams, and corners must be assessed in the creation of an optimum living space.

Doors

Just as a mouth is to a face, a door is to a building or room. Both herald our messages to the world, and it is important to recognize the commanding position that doors hold.

Doors are the passageways of ch'i. Should you return home to a cramped, dark or awkward entrance space after an exhilarating day, watch your high spirits disappear! If, on the other hand, the entrance door opens directly into a large room, your personal ch'i can be whisked away from you by the open space. Doors should not open into areas that inhibit or overwhelm.

Exterior Doors

Lucky	**Unlucky**
	Too large or too small
Facing east or south	Facing north
Statues or plants on either side of door	Not visible on the approach
Opening to a light airy space	Opening to a dark space
Providing a sense of containment	Opening in front of a staircase
Unimpeded visual access to the next room	Facing a wall within eight feet
At the end of a curved path	At the end of a straight path
	Opens to a view of another door leading outside
Level to or higher than street grade	Lower than street grade

Door Size

Oversized doors were traditionally relegated to palaces, churches and government buildings because they were designed to humble those who entered, overwhelming and undermining individual power. Oversized doors are perfect for a castle or cathedral, but not for a private home.

An undersized door has the reverse effect, for it can mash our positive energies. Small doors compress the life force and tend to make the occupants of such dwellings timid and tense.

Door Directions

"Grab your coat and get your hat, leave your troubles on the doorstep...direct your feet to the sunny side of the street." Presumedly this song was written by someone in agreement with the feng shui belief that living in a home blocked off from direct sunlight exacerbates problems. Facing east to south is best for a front door. In the morning when you leave for work, school or daily chores, a sunny scene can lift your spirits whereas west or north facing doors expose you to a drearier view.

View upon Entering

The vista just inside an entrance door is crucial in determining how energy will flow throughout a home.

A dark, cramped area or a parallel wall within a short distance of entrance will depress, inhibit or block one's ch'i.

In many cases, a staircase ascending directly in front of a door will draw ch'i away from the main area to individual bedrooms. This kind of entrance may cause individual family members to withdraw from participation in family life.

The entrance to a bi-level house is a feng shui nightmare. The entrance landing has two staircases in view. Both pathways siphon off energy and can lead to the divisiveness and dissipation of energy.

Those living with split level entrances can find it difficult to form group cohesiveness.

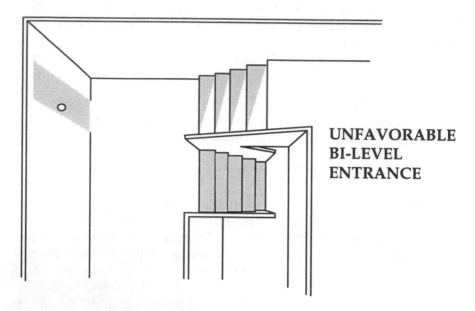

UNFAVORABLE BI-LEVEL ENTRANCE

An entrance should be well lit and provide easy access to the main areas of a home. Furniture in the foyer, like a table, chair or plant can contribute to a comfortable, secure atmosphere for anyone entering your home.

Pathways that Lead to Doors

Curved, fluid movement makes us feel good. The rocking motion of a cradle, a sweep of a hand caressing a cheek, the upward motion of a hand raising a glass in a toast--all employ curved movement. Curved pathways are more pleasant to traverse.

A pathway should prepare you for change by providing that "little bit of time" during which you make the transition to a new space.

Exit Doors Facing Each Other

Since ch'i enters a house with you through the door, it is important to continue its movement to the main gathering rooms. When the entrance door is opposite the back door, ch'i is likely to enter one door and be drawn out the other. Moreover, when ch'i flows too strongly through a space, the life force of the residents can be overpowered.

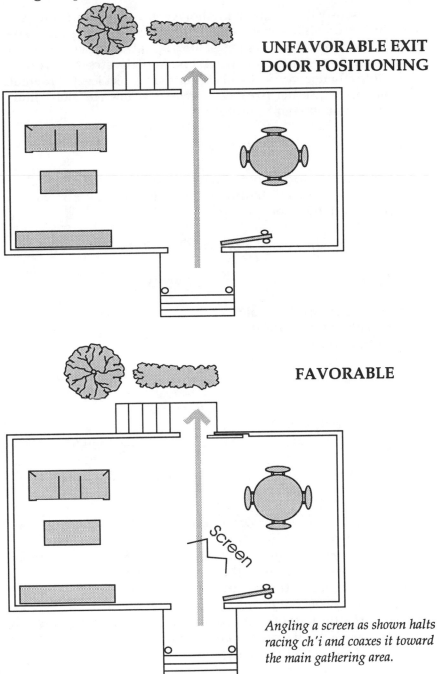

UNFAVORABLE EXIT DOOR POSITIONING

FAVORABLE

Angling a screen as shown halts racing ch'i and coaxes it toward the main gathering area.

Doors Lower than Street Grade

Like Sisyphus who, in Greek mythology, was condemned to push a huge boulder up a hill without success, leaving a dwelling and having to climb a slope each day can suggest life's uphill struggles. Feng shui also suggests that misfortune can descend from the street above down the path into a house whose door is lower than street level. Pragmatically, rain water and other street debris can flow down to such a house and can cause maintenance problems.

Interior Doors

In most contemporary homes, an unadorned opening in a wall has replaced doors. Bedrooms, bathrooms and closets are the only rooms still likely to have traditional doors.

Interior Doors or Openings

Lucky	**Unlucky**
Doors that open completely against the doorway wall (180 degrees)	Slightly misaligned
Archways	Doors in the same room that are unequal in size and directly across from each other
Opening so that most of the room can be seen	Too many doors in one area
	Unused or Awkwardly placed

How Doors Swing Open

When a theater curtain swings open, it parts with a sweeping gesture that doesn't end until the entire stage is revealed. We are immediately drawn into the scene and become oblivious to all else. In the same way a door that opens completely to reveal an entire room prepares you for the next experience. Ideally, doors should swing open a full 180 degrees. If not, a door should at least open to allow unobstructed movement through it.

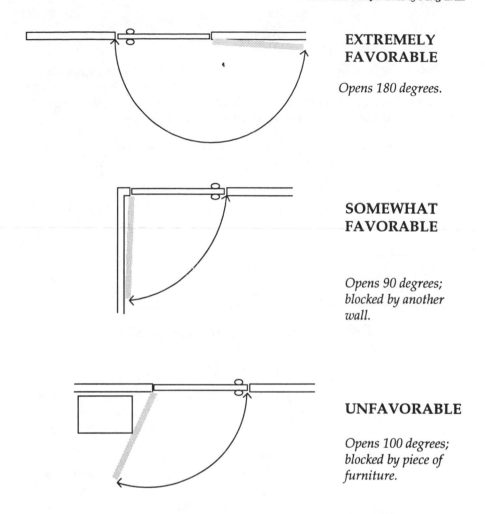

EXTREMELY FAVORABLE

Opens 180 degrees.

SOMEWHAT FAVORABLE

Opens 90 degrees; blocked by another wall.

UNFAVORABLE

Opens 100 degrees; blocked by piece of furniture.

Doors that don't open enough to allow you to view most of the room you are entering are considered unlucky. When walking through a door, you should see the widest possible view of the room entered. Your feeling of security increases when you have a clear impression of the total space.

According to feng shui, negative energy tends to collect in the empty spaces behind doors which do not open fully due to a piece of furniture, another wall or a nearby door. Instinctively, we feel better upon entering a room where there are no spaces behind the door from which we might be surprised.

Misaligned Doors

Doors slightly out of line with each other affect you in much the same way as unbalanced wheels affect an automobile. It is an insidious drain on functioning. Smooth, uninterrupted passage from room to room is a simile for smooth passage through life.

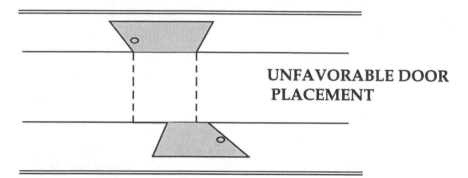

UNFAVORABLE DOOR PLACEMENT

Doors Parallel but Unequal in Size

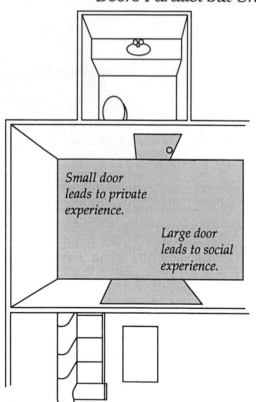

Small door leads to private experience.

Large door leads to social experience.

When two doorways face each other across a room, each door's height and width should prepare one for the next room. Doors connecting rooms should not have different heights when the rooms they connect have an equal impact on a family's life.

The only time unequal doors make any sense is when they prepare you for a different experience. If, for example, you enter a home and encounter a large opening or doorway into a main gathering room, the size of the door readies you to enter an important family space. On the other hand, a small door can prepare you to enter a small place like a closet or bathroom.

Too Many Doors in One Area

Carnivals sometimes have an attraction called "The Maze". You enter what is a series of crooked mirrored corridors and try to guess which surface is an opening and passageway to freedom. In much the same way, too many doors in one location can cause confusion, frustration or conflict.

Unused Doors or Openings

It is bad luck to have inactive areas in a home. Unused spaces can reflect losses in life or opportunities never ventured. Doors leading to unaltered bedrooms once occupied by a child can only remind one of what has been, not what could be. If a door leads into an unused area, consider using that area for meaningful activities. Always strive to create opportunities where previously there were none.

Archways

An archway frames a person passing underneath it differently than the straight overhead line of a rectangle. A curved space above the head inspires us to indulge in lofty thoughts, unlike the guillotine-like horizontal line of a rectangular door frame.

Windows

Windows are our eyes to the world. We see and are seen though them. The placement of windows and the scenes that they frame influence our lives.

Underground homes have been marketed in recent years, yet few were ever built. The public doesn't want to live underground in a windowless world.

Cultures that built dwellings with few windows, perhaps due to weather or a lack of technology, often developed strong clan systems. Not being able to look out seems to limit one's perspective of the world. The outside world remains outside the sphere of influence.

Consider the frequent use of stained glass in houses of worship. It permits light to enter but also obstructs any connection to the external world. This prompts the persons within to focus on what transpires inside.

The windows in your home are the lenses through which you view the world. What you see outside impacts your life inside. Be sure that you see what you desire.

The Windows of a Home

Lucky	**Unlucky**
Opens completely	Cannot be opened or opens partially
Frames a pleasant scene	Looks out on an airshaft, a wall, an entertainment center, a prison or cemetery
Fresh air can circulate	Opens to dank or polluted air
	Too many windows or no windows

How Windows Open

Imagine viewing the world while squinting. The view is distorted and you can suffer momentary eyestrain. A window that opens only partially limits the view and is analogous to limited opportunities.

Windows that open out involve an expansive gesture, like raising an arm to acknowledge applause. Windows that open in are more akin to a self-absorbed gesture. Opening windows may be a minor part of your daily routine, but the implication of the gesture can have a cumulative effect and become actualized through repetition alone.

Windows that don't open can, subconsciously, make a space feel like a prison. Offices with permanently sealed windows can frustrate the occupants.

The Air You Breathe

The value of fresh air to our health is obvious. Over time, polluted air outside can cause illness and affect our capacity to function well. Our brains need clean air to fuel optimum performances.

In a "sick" building, air is recirculated through heating and cooling ducts without the benefit of systematic infusions of fresh air. As a result, all germs, bacteria and mold in the system are shared by all the occupants of the building. Even in cold months, it is best to open some windows if only for a short time each day.

Too Many Windows

In the 1950's, Philip Johnson, the architect, built an all-glass house in Connecticut. This home expressed an innovative architectural style and some of its features became a model for contemporary buildings. Fish may enjoy living in a fish bowl but people do not. Consequently, glass houses did not sprout in suburbia.

More than three windows per door or entrance in each room can produce disobedient children. When I first encountered this feng shui dictum, I was puzzled until I recalled a situation that supported this theory.

In my elementary school, classrooms usually had one entire wall of windows. I was always being reprimanded by the teacher for talking with my girlfriends. While she scolded me, I would always find something outside to capture my attention. A leaf, a tree trunk, anything served to obliterate the teacher's words. In my case too many windows did indeed assist insubordination. We can reconcile this feng shui dictate by using a little psychology on misbehaving children. Just turn the children away from windows when they are being disciplined. Then you can have your windows and have obedient children too.

Windows Facing West

We are physically vulnerable by late afternoon, around 4 p.m., after having usually been active for some eight hours or more without a break. Windows that face the west allow the vivid afternoon sun to shine into the house just at the time of day when we most need a respite. When a room has windows that face west, try limiting afternoon activities that require concentration.

Ceilings

Ceilings are the skies of our interior world. Just as we associate freedom, expansiveness and endless possibilities with a broad, open sky, so is our mental condition, in part, influenced by the ceilings of our homes.

Space between the ceiling and the tallest piece of furniture is usually the only uninterrupted space in our homes. It is an area where ch'i can circulate freely. Ch'i is like a lasso swinging around our bodies, and, like the lasso, ch'i needs space to circulate. A ceiling with hanging decorations is fine in areas like restaurants where we want to keep the ch'i low over the seated diners, but in a home too many beams, suspended decorations or lights can obstruct the beneficial movement of positive ch'i.

When a ceiling slopes downward below a person's height, it can be oppressive. The feng shui suggestion that a slanted ceiling is unlucky pertains to a ceiling that slants down below eye level.

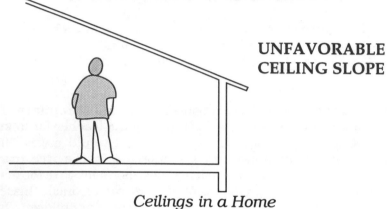

UNFAVORABLE CEILING SLOPE

Ceilings in a Home

Lucky	Unlucky
High and uninterrupted	Low or congested
	Slanted to below standing height

Exposed Beams

Beams are the skeleton of a house. Each beam plays an important role in tying together the frame of a house. A defective upright post or stud will not cause a house to come tumbling down--but watch out if a ceiling beam is impaired! Resting or seating areas located directly under a beam are considered unlucky.

Position of Beams

Lucky	Unlucky
	Over a bed, seating area or dining table

Beams Over a Bed

If a beam is positioned over a bed, the body part directly under it may experience physical difficulties. For example, if your head is directly under a beam you may suffer headaches. If a beam passes over the center of a bed and you sleep on your stomach, you may develop lower back problems.

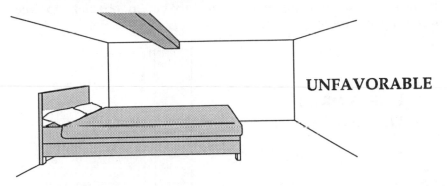

UNFAVORABLE

A ceiling beam is not the primary reason for any ailment. But, over time, an exposed beam over a bed, sofa or chair could subconsciously threaten a specific area of the body.

Beams over a sofa, a reading chair, a stove or a dining table can block out or hinder the smooth circulation of ch'i.

Beams Over a Seating Area

I once lectured where there were exposed beams in the lecture/meeting room. The owner of the center was familiar with the feng shui dictate that beams over seating areas might bring misfortune to her fledgling business. The exposed beams crossed the ceiling every eighteen inches; thus almost everyone in the room would be under a beam.

I alleviated her fears by explaining why this dictate did not apply to her situation. In ancient China very few ceilings soared 20 feet high as hers did. The height of the ceiling allowed ch'i to flow uninterruptedly and mitigated the oppressive feeling that a low hanging, exposed beam might produce.

It is important to interpret all feng shui instructions in light of contemporary realities. What once made sense might not make sense today.

Corners

There are no lucky or unlucky corners; however, there can be corners positioned inappropriately within a room. Corners redirect movement. Sometimes a wall beam concealing a pipe will protrude into a room. This interruption in the surface of a wall is, at the very least, a decorating challenge. A wall protrusion can also prevent a door from swinging open completely or it can be an obstacle to free movement from room to room.

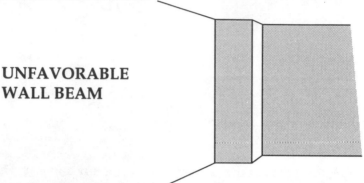

UNFAVORABLE WALL BEAM

The corners of a room, like the corners of a mind, need to be accessible so that they do not become inactive. Integrate corners of a room into the rest of a space so that the energy's momentum can circulate uninterrupted and thus dead spaces (analogous to wasted talents) cease to exist.

Corners, Indoors and Outdoors

Lucky	Unlucky
Visually integrated into the overall decor	Unincorporated in an overall scheme

Color

The way we color our world reflects how we feel. The visual statement made by the color of your clothes influences the way others perceive you. Certain colors evoke specific emotions. In many instances, the feelings generated by a color reflect where these colors are found in the natural world. Before selecting the colors you want to live with, consider their intrinsic messages.

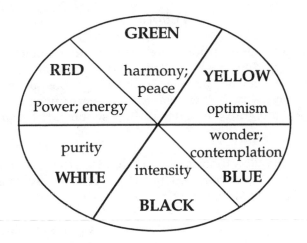

Red

Red exists sparingly in nature. Only some plants bud to red. Occasionally a streak of red appears as one color in a dramatic sky. Soil is red only when specific mineral deposits are present. It is an extraordinary color which stimulates a strong response. Power, potency and intensity are a few interpretations of red.

Red also represents energy and inspires action. Fire glows red, we "see red" when angry and when we want to have fun we "paint the town red." We don't use the color red to create a severe, contemplative atmosphere. In fact, owners of red automobiles are issued more traffic tickets than owners of any other color car.

Red should be used when seeking power or attention. Whenever I lecture, I always wear something red to bring me energy and give me power. In a field of many colors, red is often the first color we see. It jumps out at us. Red is noticed. Red equals active energy.

Green

Green is in the center of the color spectrum. It is a color we see often in nature, and it emits feelings of harmony, freshness and peace. Green soothes the spirit. In feng shui, green is the color of family and knowledge.

I once wrote a paper in college on the use of color in mental institutions. I learned that a light shade of green produced a calming effect on patients. This supported a feng shui hypothesis--that green helps us to feel connected, tranquil and safe.

Yellow

We could not exist without the sun. Some ancient cultures worshipped its golden glow. Yellow is the color of the sun's life sustaining power, so we perceive it as a symbol for brightness, longevity and mystery. Yellow generates cheerfulness like a sunny day, and, when integrated in a decorating scheme, the room exudes optimism.

Gold is a noble yellow that represents dignity, respect and richness. In China, gold robes were reserved for the imperial family. Gold evokes a more formal atmosphere than does its cousin yellow.

In feng shui, both yellow and red are colors that stimulate actualization. Yellow contributes to an elevated mental state and when we feel good, we are more likely to bring out the best.

Blue

Although blue is not a primary color, its presence in our natural world has given it a special place. Most of the earth is covered with the color blue. The unknown depths of oceans, lakes and rivers elicit our awe and wonder. Water evokes contemplation of the enigma of life.

Blue, like the seas, can elicit a sense of isolation, but it can also be perceived as an exaltation of selfhood. Who but the brave will venture out to sea? The seas are the ultimate challenge to the inner person. Perhaps blue is popular in men's clothing because it implies a rugged individualism.

White or Black

White represents the absence of all color while black absorbs them all. In both cases they represent extremes. Cultures have assigned intense meaning to these extremes.

The Chinese wear white for a funeral color, while Westerners wear black. It may be that white represents release of the mortal self to the cosmos, while black represents the absorption of grief.

These colors must touch emotional chords within us, considering their specific use for cultural rituals. Does the white of a bride's gown represent purity and a willingness to be passive and careful in her interaction with the world? Does a groom's black tuxedo allow him more freedom in his behavior? Perhaps black, the color that absorbs all around it, is a symbol for assuming responsibility.

If we decorate our living spaces primarily in black and white, we draw attention to other details and make them more significant. For example, colorful paintings hung on the walls of an all-white room bring our eyes to this display of talent. Moreover, if a room lacks other focal points, people become the center of attention in monochromatic black and white interiors. This may or may not be appropriate.

One of my clients enjoyed dating relaxed, down-home kind of guys. She didn't understand why her dates did not like spending time at her home. As soon as I saw her all white living room, I knew that it was unappealing to those who would rather lounge around with their feet up. We "cured" this by placing colorful blankets and pillows on the sofa and layering small patterned area rugs over the white carpeted floors.

Shades and Mixes of Color

The orange/saffron robes of the Buddhist monks combine the mysticism of the color yellow with the power implicit in red. The choice of purple in ancient royal fashions employs the energy invoked by red mixed with the limitlessness suggested by the color blue. Combine colors to help realize your goals.

In my writing room, for example, I laid purple, red and black tiles in a spiral design. The shape of the spiral and the choice of colors reflect my aspiration. Purple represents infinite wisdom, red charges my mental energy, the black reminds me to absorb as much knowledge as possible, and the spiral represents the connection we have to all things in the hierarchy of life and the infinite journey of knowledge.

Part II

A *Room to Room Guide*

Walls define interior space and create a womb that cradles our desires. A well-designed space can give birth to life's goals. Now that we have investigated the general areas that can alter one's life experience, it is time to learn how to manipulate our individual living spaces so as to optimize their feng shui quotient.

One of the reasons that I fell in love with feng shui was that its inventory of cures for imperfect situations can easily be implemented with inexpensive solutions. In the vast majority of cases, structural changes are not required, and I have resorted to suggesting architectural alterations in a mere handful of cases.

The first step is to define a room's use. The key to creating a successful space is an awareness of who will use the room, what kinds of activities will be central to that room, and when it will be used. Only after you have outlined "Who, What and When" can you begin to organize the space.

Before reading the following chapters, use these guidelines to assist in evaluating your needs.

1. Who will use the space? List in order of importance the people who will be affected by this space. A bedroom's occupant is clearly its most important person, while a gathering room might have a number of people whose needs should be considered.

2. What activities will take place in this room? Will a space serve only one purpose or will more than one function be integrated into it? Is a dining room just for eating or does it double as a catch-all for a family's mail or paperwork? Does a bedroom double as a study, work area or dressing room? Is the room that houses the family's television set also used for social gatherings and does it have comfortable seating for both activities? Make a list of the activities generated in each room.

3. When will a space be occupied? The time of day in which a room is used influences the positioning of the furniture and other accessories. For example, a kitchen is normally used in the morning and at the end of the day while a teenager's bedroom is primarily used in the late afternoon.

With a well-defined sense of your personal requirements, you are ready to tackle the task of improving your life, room by room.

Chapter Six

First Impressions

Although you can't judge a book by its cover, some are ignored because their covers fail to entice. The clothes we choose to wear often indicate how we wish to be perceived. In the same way, first impressions of a space contribute to how we and others will experience it.

I live in a small, friendly neighborhood. It is not uncommon to see groups of neighbors conversing in the middle of our one-lane sand roads. However, one neighbor clearly prefers to remain apart and has successfully generated a first impression that causes the rest of us to stay away. Their "stop signs" include:

1. No clearly defined path to an entrance door;
2. Identical front and back doors;
3. Curtains drawn all the time;
4. Lack of embellishments next to either entrance door.

The lack of a clear pathway to an entrance door causes uncertainty for an approaching visitor. And if there is no clearly defined front door, additional confusion is spawned. Drawn curtains, like closed eyes, communicate a desire for privacy and the lack of color, vegetation, light or objects near a door does not entice a visitor to approach. These signals are loud and clear; everyone stays away.

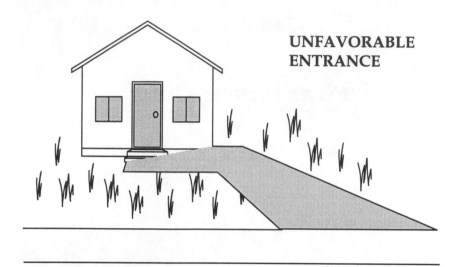

UNFAVORABLE ENTRANCE

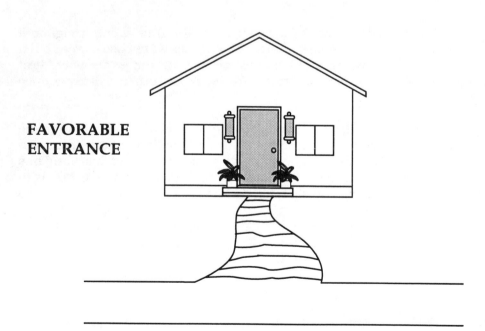

FAVORABLE ENTRANCE

You can also become what you see. Just as your entrance sends a message, the buildings opposite your front door can influence your life. Avoid living across the street from or too near to prisons, entertainment centers or cemeteries. They can either siphon off your own ch'i or reflect negative energy back to you. Although they do not emit unfavorable ch'i, houses of worship are also to be eschewed. They are designed, for the most part, to inspire awe and overwhelm the individual. Thus, houses of worship can drain away our personal ch'i.

In contemporary buildings, many rooms are defined by furniture placement. Examining the number of rooms that have doors gives a partial view of family structure. The Victorian life-style, for example, was formal and circumspect and having doors for every room closed each to casual observation. Their use of doors reflects their society's mores. Today very little is taboo and only bedrooms and bathrooms have doors that shut.

The amount of floor space allocated to an area influences its function. One wonders whether the advent of narrow galley kitchens was the brainchild of a marketing department of the frozen food industry! Such a kitchen clearly says that more than one's a crowd. No wonder we need prepared foods and labor-saving gadgets when we are provided with only enough space for one person to work comfortably. Either the cook is sequestered in the kitchen, isolated from the rest of the family, or everyone must constantly dodge each other if congregated therein.

Color sets the emotional tone for a room. How many libraries have brightly painted walls and patterned floors? The selection of muted tones encourages thoughtful, respectful behavior. On the other hand, children's rooms animated with bright colors and patterns encourage a high energy level. A dark somber room would not meet the needs of most children.

The notion of love at first sight attests to the overwhelming impact an initial impression can have on one. First impressions can affect behavior; they can stimulate a positive frame of mind or create bad vibes. Creating auspicious first impressions will prompt others to find you or your living space appealing.

When your room emits the feeling you intended and reflects your goals at first glance, you have already begun to achieve your desires.

Guidelines for Front Entrances

Positive	**Negative**
Clearly defined, curved walkways	Straight or nonexistent walkway
Enhanced with well tended vegetation	Over-run or sparse vegetation
Entrance situated at ground level or elevated from street	Facing the base of a hill or mountain
	Facing power lines, a church or a cemetery
Facing east or south	Facing north
	At a T-juncture
Opening to a well-defined place	Opening in a direct line to another door

Chapter Seven

Gathering Rooms

In many homes today the central family meeting room is not the living room. It is the room called the den, family room or great room. The family spends its leisure time in this room which functions as the center of a home or the main gathering room. Like the heart in a body, it is the chamber where the family's vitality flows and where collective energies can be nourished in an inviting, safe and appropriate space.

After you have defined which area should function as a main gathering room, make a list of additional gathering spaces. A list of gathering places might look like this:

Main Gathering Room- The room where the family meets daily to engage in a variety of activities.

Formal Gathering Room-A space where important or formal events take place.

Special Gathering Room- A room where the family engages in one specific activity. For example: swimming, ping-pong, pool or games for the children.

Tertiary Gathering Areas-A place to meet with trades people, tutors or persons who are not friends or relatives. The need for this kind of space has been greatly reduced over the years by a more egalitarian life-style.

Even though these rooms will function differently, all of the same criteria should be addressed in designing the rooms' layouts.

1. Who uses this room? Some additional questions can be: Should there be a "power" seat or seats in this room? How many people typically use this room? What will the optimum capacity be for this space?

2. When is the room used? Do the activities here take place during the day or at night?

3. What activities will take place in this room? How valuable is this room in sustaining a healthy family life?

Main Gathering Room

A main gathering room should be inviting, beckoning family and friends inside. It should be comfortable and decorated to express the family's taste and interests. In the vernacular of feng shui, these decorations are often called "power symbols" because they communicate that which is important in the family's lives and validates its choices.

The most responsible members of a family should have seats that face a room's entrance door. Here the family's "guardian" can see who enters and can be seen by anyone who comes in. One is likely to assume a role of importance when given a place of importance.

A room's wealth corner is where symbols of success, abundance or good fortune are displayed. It should be located at the "safest" point of a room; usually the furthest corner from an entrance door. This is perhaps a remnant of times when it was essential to see a predator's approach and have sufficient time to react. According to feng shui's belief, symbols of financial success in a wealth corner can enhance our ability to accrue wealth. Place objects in this corner that represent things that you value.

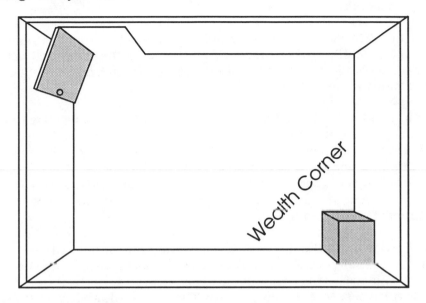

A wealth corner should have solid walls. Lacking that, a floor plant, fish tank lamp or screen can be strategically placed in the area to provide grounding and focus. Do not hang a mirror in this corner for it will tend to disperse fortune. Adorn the windows in this area with curtains, shades or divider screens so that the ch'i imbued in your valuables will not fly out through the window.

I'm concerned that young people who watch television will duplicate the furniture arrangement depicted in TV homes. Here straight passageways are designed so that actors can make flourishing entrances and exits. Straight passageways in a home can induce both people and ch'i to fly through a room. Moreover, a stage set for television has open-ended seating because close intimate seating would destroy camera angles. No one would be able to converse eye-to-eye with the TV-type arrangements. Thus, these are usually the worst possible ones to duplicate in real life.

Providing gently curving passageways for ch'i creates an atmosphere of calm and promotes family harmony. Avoid straight pathways from the door of the main gathering room to other rooms. Furniture should not be positioned where it will obstruct an entrance. Seating should be close and intimate so that no one will feel out of the mainstream.

A southeast exposure is favorable, and the main gathering room should be well lit, especially at night. Like the light of a lighthouse, its ch'i should draw all to port.

The main gathering room should be accessible from the home's most frequently used entrance and preferably on the same level as the entrance. Walking up or down stairs in order to reach a gathering area dissipates some of its appeal.

It should also be self-contained. If the room does not have four walls, strategic placement of a screen, plant, sculpture or a high piece of furniture can help to create a nest-like atmosphere. Much contemporary architecture features an open floor plan. Airy, larger spaces may at first seem appealing, but there is a tendency to be drawn away, even in thought, from a room's activities when you are visually attracted to another space.

Provide an inviting, nurturing, relaxing atmosphere where your family can congregate. Avoid extreme monochromatic schemes; it over-emphasizes the people in the room. Georgia O'Keefe, the painter, decorated her studio totally in white. The floor, walls and ceilings were painted white and all the furniture was draped with white sheets. This created a living canvas upon which any object was framed and became larger than life. Attention was drawn to any object or person placed in her living canvas. Excessive pressure is placed upon the occupants when their physical beings are made conspicuous by a stark environment. However, refrain also from clutter and a melange of furniture with a variety of heights, shapes and styles. Too many objects can overwhelm an individual's ch'i. Find a happy medium that expresses your aesthetics even as it harmonizes the relationship between you and your living space.

Auxiliary Gathering Rooms

Contemporary life is fraught with ambiguity. Survival does not require the time and effort that it once did, and we have developed a host of leisure activities to fill the resulting gap. A prime example of this is television. Unfortunately, many television programs provide empty entertainment, much like non-nutritious filler in a hamburger, and we have not improved our lives by its inclusion.

We attach status to the amount of space in a home. No longer is it satisfactory to have only one gathering room as many of our grandparents did. These rooms were noisy and sometimes a bit chaotic, but we always felt secure within our family's unity. Children and adults interacted and shared the same gathering space like several flower petals occupying a single stem.

When there are additional gathering rooms in a home, be sure that these separate areas contribute to family life. If a children's playroom exists, do not allow it to prevent a healthy interaction between adult and child. If a gathering room exists to provide space or a single activity like swimming, billiards or card-playing, be sure it can be used by all family members whether they are participating in the activity or not. Do not allow it to become an alienating element in the family structure.

Guidelines for Main and Auxiliary Gathering Rooms

Positive	Negative
Having visible partitions	No discernible boundaries
Closed seating arrangements	Seating facing one direction
Accessible from the main entrance	Down a narrow hallway or on a different level from main entrance
Well-lit day or night	Darkened corners or areas
A wealth corner	Too stark or cluttered
Most seating backed by a wall	Exposed beams over seating areas

A family's strength is more than the sum of its individual parts. Nurturing a quality space in which we can share our lives can provide an individual with the support needed to thrive.

Chapter Eight

The Family Hearth

In the hierarchy of life's essentials, nourishment is extremely important. Survival is possible without shelter, clothing or even human contact, but impossible without food and water. The creation of a peaceful, supportive atmosphere in which to dine will result in emotional, spiritual, and physical benefits.

You Are <u>Where</u> You Eat

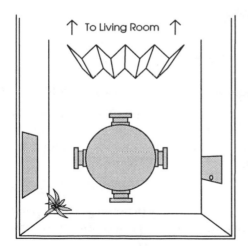

One should dine in a specific room where the atmosphere is as important as the food itself. The hearth is, in many ways, the heart of a home. A dining area that is not its own contained space should be clearly defined by screens, plants or other room dividers. Although some natural light should filter in, it is important to have solid walls or wall facsimiles so that, when diners are seated at a table, their backs face a solid support.

The shape of a dining room table should encourage conversation and intimacy. Each person should be included in a circle of close communion while comfortable in a niche of their own. A dining room table is most appropriate when it accommodates the number of people that typically use it. A table that seats six persons is all right for a family of four but too big for a family of two.

Round, octagonal and oval shapes are preferable. It is awkward to converse at a long rectangular or large square table. A table's width should accommodate two table settings with enough space in between for serving plates. If you have to stand up to pass dishes across the table, it is too wide.

A person's location at a table indicates their position in the family hierarchy and, sometimes, their self-esteem. The person ultimately responsible for the family's well-being should face the entrance door. In today's more egalitarian households, both mother and father often sit next to each other in that favored position.

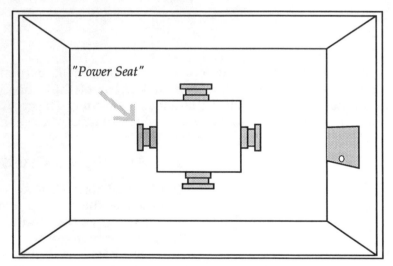

The table should be the dining room's main focus. The pulse of this room is the food and persons present. A few objects reflecting a family's tastes and values can be used as decoration as long as they do not distract from the central focus. We need little more than diners, dinnerware and food in a dining area.

Just as sleep revitalizes our bodies after a day of activity, time spent in the dining room provides a sense of unity and emotional nourishment for family members after a day spent apart.

Guidelines for Dining Rooms

Positive	**Negative**
Dining in a separate room or clearly defined area	Dining in an open area within a room
A reasonable number of windows	Too many windows and doors
Round, octagonal or oval table	A long rectangle or unusually large square table
A few cherished art objects	Clutter

The Kitchen

Food gives us more than physical nourishment; it influences our emotions and behavior. Healthy, fresh, vital foods imbue us with similar qualities. Our attitude when we prepare food can affect the benefit the food will have to those who eat it. If we are what we eat, then the setting in which a cook prepares food is central to our self-actualization. Kitchens are the chambers in which we store and prepare the nourishment that should also provide us with warmth, power and love.

The kitchen is the only place in a home where fire and water coexist. In the Chinese chart of the five elements (earth, wood, water, metal and fire) fire and water are considered to be incompatible when placed in close proximity. Water quells fire, so the sink should not be next to the stove. However, the sink should not be across the room from the stove, making it necessary for the cook to cross floor space when transferring hot pots to the sink. The sink and stove can be across a counter top from one another. Placing these two elements close but not next to each other is ideal.

The placement of kitchen appliances is critical. The Chinese believe that the stove should not be against a north wall because the severest weather sweeps in from the north. Since wood was used as a cooking fuel, extra work was required to keep a stove hot when it backed up to a north wall. Even today when most of us heat with gas or electricity, we must be conscious of the extra energy required to fuel a stove placed against the home's coldest wall.

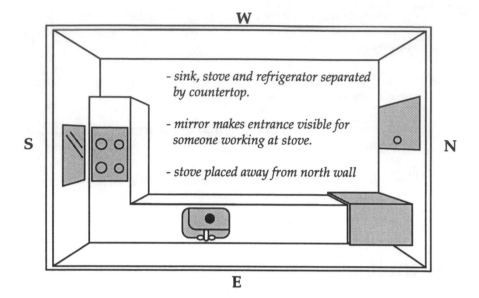

W

- sink, stove and refrigerator separated
  by countertop.

- mirror makes entrance visible for
  someone working at stove.

- stove placed away from north wall

S

N

E

FAVORABLE KITCHEN
ARRANGEMENT

Where is the hub of activity in your kitchen? Which surfaces, appliances and conveniences do you use most often? Depending on family food preferences and season of the year, the location and preparation procedures may vary. Since I am a vegetarian, I am more often stationed with my cutting board at the sink than at any other area in my kitchen. For others, the stove is the most frequently-used food preparation surface. In any case, it is critical for the cook to be able to see anyone who enters. Identify your primary cooking station to help determine how to best utilize feng shui's suggestions.

A well-lit, roomy cooking station should be central in a kitchen. Even the most inspired cook will soon get discouraged without enough light in a room with which to create. It is critical for the cook to be able to see any person who enters the kitchen. If a kitchen doorway cannot be seen from a cook's primary work area, a mirror can be positioned to reflect such an entrance.

A kitchen should have a flexible lighting system. Overhead ceiling lights can cause shadows over a work-station. Mount lighting beneath the overhead cabinets or on walls behind the counters to eliminate this problem.

Kitchen walls should not share bathroom walls. The tainted waters of the bathroom are considered unlucky when situated next to the food preparation room.

Guidelines for Kitchens

Positive	**Negative**
A contained space	Lacking three defining partitions
Stove on an east or south wall	Stove on the north wall
Appropriately lit work space near sink and stove	Only ceiling lighting fixtures
An entrance door that can be seen while cooking	Having one wall common with a bathroom

In many ways, food preparation is a meditation and it should be executed in a beautiful, safe, functional space.

Chapter Nine

A Space of One's Own

Having a space of our own is an unparalleled joy. This private space should be one of total safety where our internal powers can be restored. For most, the bedroom becomes this special place and we must pay careful attention to how we shape our private spaces.

Bedrooms

One's bedroom is a retreat from the shared activity rooms and a refuge from routine daily tasks. One should feel totally safe and completely at ease here.

The placement of the bed should be the first consideration when planning this room, for this is where both the body and soul are recharged. The head of the bed should back up to a solid wall. Without a wall behind us, we may feel vulnerable and a peaceful state of relaxation can be undermined. We should be able to see our bedroom's entrance door while sitting in bed without having to strain or twist in order to view who is entering. Although the door should be seen from the bed without having to turn the head more than 90 degrees, it should not be in direct line with the entrance door, for this might startle the person in bed whenever someone enters the room.

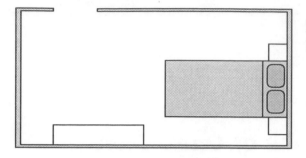

FAVORABLE BED POSITIONING

Door can be seen without turning head 45 degrees while in bed.

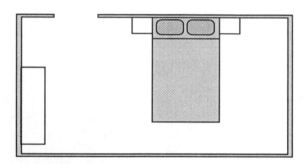

UNFAVORABLE BED POSITIONING

Door can't be seen without turning head at more than a 45 degree angle.

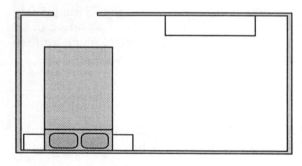

UNFAVORABLE BED POSITIONING

Bed is in direct line with the entrance door.

Do not place a bed directly under a beam, a light fixture, a paddle fan or any other hanging object. If the room is small and such placement is unavoidable, be sure that your head is positioned as far away as possible from such objects. A weakness can develop in the body part over which a beam is positioned. For example, if there is a beam over the center of your bed, you may develop stomach problems.

Another feng shui rule dictates that it is unlucky to sleep under a slanted ceiling. Although the Chinese believe that all slanting ceilings or shed roof lines are negative, I am convinced that they were thought to be negative because few ceilings were very high. Today's technology makes it less expensive to build higher roofs, and thus elevated slanted ceilings seldom seem as claustrophobic. Even when there is sufficient height, it is still best to avoid sleeping under the lower end of any slanted ceiling. The thrust of a downward line can subconsciously be perceived as oppressive.

Although mirrors are solutions to many feng shui ills, mirrors should be kept to a minimum in bedrooms. Certainly one should not be positioned directly across from your waking self. Mirrors in that position objectify our sense of self during the transition from sleep to wakefulness. This period is fragile because we are more reactive and sensitive to what we see. Some of us need hours before we feel that we are fully awake. Seeing yourself in a mirror when you are not completely alert can undermine a serene state of mind.

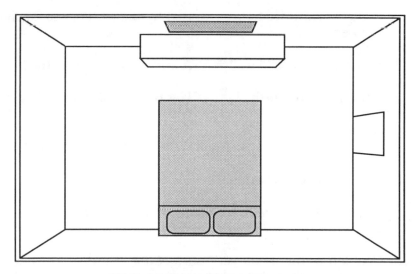

UNFAVORABLE MIRROR
POSITIONING

Only pleasant activities should take place in a bedroom. Because of lack of space, I am aware that many people in small apartments use their bedrooms as offices, workshops or television rooms. Often this can sabotage the peaceful atmosphere that should prevail in this room. Other activities requiring privacy, such as reading or listening to music, can be appropriate in a bedroom, as long as they do not require too much active (yang) energy.

The head of the family usually occupies the largest bedroom. This room should be in the guardian's position, accessible to the other bedrooms but at the same time with a buffer zone at its entrance. The colors of the master bedroom should contribute to a feeling of tranquillity. More important than this room's size is its potential for balanced ch'i. Modern homes with the master bedroom in a separate wing are, in many cases, contributing to the disintegration of the family unit. How can parents maintain their traditional role as leaders when they are removed from the position of guardian?

Guidelines for Bedrooms

Lucky	**Unlucky**
Used only as a retreat	Needing this space for work-related activities
A visible entrance from the bed	Bed in line with entrance door
Bed against a solid wall	A mirror across from the bed
Facing east or north	Low part of a slanted ceiling over bed
	A ceiling beam over a bed

Auxiliary Private Spaces

It is preferable to have separate rooms at home for work and leisure activities.

The position of the main work surface (be it a desk, laboratory counter or exercise center) should follow the same guidelines as those for the bed in a bedroom. But there are additional criteria.

When working at a writing surface the light source should cross the shoulder of the non-prominent hand. Therefore, if you are right-handed, the light should shine over your left shoulder and, if you are left-handed, over your right shoulder.

Inspirational or beloved art and objects are appropriate in this setting. Over my writing desk I have a picture of my grandmother; she reminds me that the sum of a life is ultimately measured by one's impact on future generations. I also have drawings done by women who live in the foothills of the Himalayas; they remind me of the creative juices that flow throughout all women in this world. These pictures help to kindle my determination and creativity.

Auxiliary private spaces should both charge your energy and soothe your spirit. Balancing active energy (yang) and passive energy (yin) is imperative. I keep a drum set in my writing room; after hours of thinking, cogitating and analyzing, I find that I can use the drums to release physical energy by pounding away. A popular toy for executives consists of several swinging balls that hang on separate cords. This desktop plaything attempts to bring yang energy to an area that is normally yin.

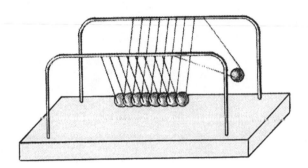

Avoid having any pathways behind a chair in your work space. Passages behind our seating areas make us feel uncomfortable and can siphon off our positive ch'i. If unavoidable, place a mirror on the facing wall to reflect what is behind your back.

Guidelines for Home Work Spaces

Positive	**Negative**
Work station positioned with a view of entrance door	Work station in a direct line with entrance door
Unobstructed light source	Exposed ceiling beam across work station
Both yin and yang areas	Work stations under lowest part of a slanted ceiling
Art objects that inspire	Pathway behind work station's chair

Chapter Ten

Private Areas

The place where we clean and care for our bodies often reflects the culture's mores as well as its technical achievements.

The ways in which we perform our personal chores are often echoed by our emotional and physical well-being. A person whose appearance suggests lack of care reveals a lack of self-esteem. We must pay full attention to the design and layout of these private spaces to bring out the best in ourselves.

A sink, toilet and tub/shower comprise the principal pieces of equipment in this space. Although many homes are built with all three in one room, it is far better for them to be separated. Ideally, these three items should be separated by a wall or partition from one another. If this is not possible, place the sink and toilet in one room and the tub/shower in another.

The pleasure of luxuriating in a tub of hot water includes the feeling that negativity seems to melt away while we soak in the steaming liquid. Even a shower helps as water connects us to our earliest environment. Enveloped within its shield, we are cleansed in more ways than merely hygienic.

The Japanese have a long history of using one room exclusively for bathing. Pitchers of hot water are poured over a bather while he relaxes in a steaming tub until tension seems to disappear. The Orthodox Jewish ritual of the Mikvah, a precursor to the ritual of baptism, uses bathing as a symbol for absolution. A Mikvah is sometimes held in a ritual bathhouse where religious brides-to-be traditionally purify themselves prior to their weddings. Here cleanliness is indeed next to godliness.

Tranquillity, privacy and comfort are three necessary ingredients for a bathing area. The space should put you profoundly at ease. If you can afford only one luxury in your home, provide a separate room in which to bathe. If there are many people in the household, separating the shower/tub area from the sink and toilet area may be an even higher priority. A separate room or glass enclosures or shower curtains that can be zipped or snapped to form a cloth wall can all insure a feeling of privacy.

The mirror you use when you comb your hair, shave your face or apply make-up need not be over a sink. I prefer to gaze out the window over my sink and let my mind wander while I brush my teeth. Other chores that require a mirrored surface may be dignified by sitting down at a dressing table or made easier by placing the mirror where you are not required to lean over a counter top.

Plumbing fixtures are like the organs in our body. Their condition can echo our health. Like a small unattended leak, neglected conditions can snowball into a disaster. Sinks, toilets and tub or shower stalls that are not in good working order should be fixed immediately. Feng shui insists that leaky plumbing is a sign of bleeding finances. Your personal wealth is your body. If you ignore caring for the place where you attend to personal hygiene, you might also disregard looking after other segments of your life.

A toilet should not be placed directly in line with the entrance door. If it is so located, place a barrier like a plant, curtain or shelving between the toilet and the door.

A bathroom needs natural ventilation. Windows can be placed anywhere except in areas which deprive one of privacy. Relaxing while performing intimate bodily functions in the bathroom is more difficult when there is a chance, however slight, that we might be observed.

A bathroom should never be positioned so that the door opens into a common room, especially the kitchen. Feng shui is often understood on an intuitive level. For example, in the county where I live, building codes rule out building a bathroom which opens into a kitchen. It is best if a bathroom is tucked away down a hall or around the bend from rooms that are frequently occupied. Even a bathroom next to a bedroom should have a separation like a hallway, closet or large piece of furniture against the common wall. I have recently seen some disastrous house plans that feature open areas above the eight foot walls that separate the master bath from the master bedroom. I can only imagine what negative consequences it could have on a marriage.

Don't relegate this room to secondary status. We are inclined to use the bathroom as a catch-all repository. We often see bottles and jars piled on bathroom counter tops, towels thrown over shower curtain rods to dry, or yesterday's clothing scattered here and there. Create a space for private functions that encourages and supports the best self-care.

Guidelines for Bathrooms

Positive	**Negative**
Separating shower/tub area	A door adjacent to a communal room
Clean and organized	Leaky plumbing
Ventilation to the outside	Direct view of a toilet from the entrance door

Chapter Eleven

Neighborhoods

The adage in real estate circles, "Buy the worst house in the best neighborhood" implies that even the humblest handyman's special can be transformed into something valuable when it sits in a flourishing area.

Excellence inspires us to aspire towards the highest level, and, indeed, what surrounds your life penetrates its borders.

Prisons, factories, busy entertainment centers, houses of worship and, in some cases, schools can introduce imperfect energy to a neighborhood of homes. The energy from these establishments either overwhelms the appropriate pace of family life or it introduces a negative energy to the area.

Consider shape as well as the condition and activity of adjacent buildings. Buildings that tower over yours are ominous and can harm an otherwise positive feng shui quotient.

A chimney that spews smoke and ash into the air over a home is like a burning match ready to ignite and destroy. The facade of a broad, tall building looming over yours is like an obstacle that cannot be circumvented. In some cases, the taller building simply blocks out sunlight.

In my oceanside neighborhood, most of the homes are unpretentious single-story structures. However, as the area becomes "discovered", more affluent families build homes to replace the original cottages with upscale houses that soar as high in the sky as the building codes will allow. I have watched with trepidation as these new houses cast shadows on the buildings and lives of those living nearby.

"Good fences make good neighbors." These lines penned by Robert Frost echo positive feng shui principles. In China, homes are likely to have a gate or an enclosed portion of property to hold in what is dear as well as keep out what is undesirable. A clear border around a property imparts security even as it marks territory. Fences can be made of wood, stone, metal, foliage or topographical features, and are to a home what a frame is to a painting. When we frame something, we emphasize its importance and highlight its existence.

Guidelines for Neighborhoods

Positive	**Negative**
Flourishing and well-maintained	Towering structures that face yours
Designated property perimeters	Structures that block the sunlight
	Structures that house activities which produce excess energy

In a heap of coal even a diamond can look bleak whereas even a hunk of coal in a setting of gold can look thrilling. Your home does not exist in a vacuum. It is preferable for your neighborhood to reflect what is best for you.

Chapter Twelve

How to Cure Your Living Space

Sometimes the distance between knowledge and its application can seem as wide as the Grand Canyon. To cure the ills in a living space you need to establish guidelines so that you can begin traversing the distance between what is and what is wanted.

Identifying goals is the first step toward coming up with answers. No two persons have the same desires, interests or set of circumstances, so there is no single correct way to arrange a space. A living space must be customized to dove-tail with specific needs. Renting a furnished apartment or buying a model home is about as comfortable as wearing someone else's shoes. What may have worked yesterday could need adjusting today. Be aware of how your needs are evolving and update your living space accordingly. In order to steer your life down the correct path, you have to chart the course.

The following questions are offered as a guide to help you uncover the profound influences in your life. Search your heart for answers. Do not be swayed by convention.

Establishing Priorities

1. What are my goals? What do I hope to achieve in my home life? Relaxation-excellence-contentment-a cohesive family life-inspiration, etc. Make up two lists, one for long term and one for short term goals.

2. Who owns each room? Which family member has responsibility, power or vested interest in each room? The parents in a family dining room or a child in his or her bedroom? Does an occasional visitor or a family member need a separate extra bedroom?

After uncovering specific individual needs, turn your attention to the living space. Mentally remove all furniture and accessories from each room and use the following outline to ensure that you have sufficient knowledge about your home and neighborhood to help make changes that will benefit your life.

How to Evaluate Your Living Space

1. Consider the area's history. Start with general information about the people, events and environment. Research the origin and history of the neighborhood by querying neighbors, local merchants, letter carriers, etc. A picture of the spirit and karma of the region will emerge. If it is mostly positive, relax and bask in its supportive light. If negative, you can alter its impact by making cosmic amends. I built a small pond in the front of my home for two reasons--water brings good luck and, since the area's swamps were drained to create dry land for homes, my pond salutes the original land.

    If a home has been occupied by others, their good and bad actions can leave wisps of influence not unlike the trailing vapors of an airplane.

    The influence of past actions wanes with the passage of time unless the incident was particularly traumatic. Suicides, abnormal deaths or serious accidents leave a lingering trail in the aura of a place. If appropriate, rate your area on a plus or minus scale for karma.

2.   Make an inventory of natural and man-made topo-
       graphic features. (hills, buildings, streets, bodies of
       water, etc.) Make a map to help you pinpoint your
       home's location. It is helpful to indicate the direction of
       the prevailing winds.

3.   Locate the four directions. East, west, north and
       south.

4.   Draw the overall shape of the house on the plot of land,
       indicating pathways and driveways.

5.   Diagram each room separately. List the expected
       activities that will be central to the room's function.

6.   Include architectural details in the individual room
       plan. Include windows, beams, fireplaces, wall protru-
       sions and doors.

7.   Consider essential paths of ch'i through a room.

8.   Indicate natural as well as man-made sources of light.
       Locate the direction of light from windows. Perma-
       nently attached lighting fixtures should be indicated
       on your plan. Lamps and movable fixtures can be
       placed after the furniture is positioned.

9.   Determine the best location for furniture. Place furni-
       ture according to the guidelines in the chapters on each
       individual room. Avoid placing any in the pathways
       of ch'i.

10.   Imagine colors that would benefit each setting and list
       them next to each room's floor plan. Remember to
       select a color that conveys a message that is appropri-
       ate for the space.

11.   Place symbols in appropriate places. Visualize each
       room with the people who will occupy it. A room's
       beauty lies also in its ability to inspire, so be sure to fill
       each room with symbols that will kindle one's internal
       flame. For example, a framed photograph of a memor-
       able holiday feast might inspire a cook to consider each
       meal as an event. Trophies adorning a casual
       gathering room can signal a family's pride in the

achievements of it's members. A cherished antique, a musical instrument, a good luck symbol or a beautiful painting can spark positive energy.

Just as the earth rotates and exposes a different side to the sun each hour of the day, so do our lives evolve, making what is suitable for one decade inappropriate for the next. It is important to re-evaluate our direction and renovate our living spaces to accommodate these changes. As we spin through the seasons of our lives, we must discover the best in each phase. Yearning for the past or wishing for the future will not help us to triumph in the present.

Ten Guidelines to Follow

1. Create a separation between the entrance foyer and the rest of the interior space. Transition time is needed from the exterior world into our homes.

2. Provide clear-cut pathways both within each room and from room to room. Distinct passageways make one feel secure.

3. Represent nature in your home with the five elements: water, fire, metal, wood and earth. These remind us of our connection to the whole earth and they nurture a sense of well-being.

4. Have important seating areas in your home face windows that look east or south. Sunlight promotes optimism.

5. Arrange your bed so that you can see any person who enters the room without having to turn your head more than 45 degrees. You do not want to be startled when you are trying to relax.

6. Furnish your home with both yin lines (curved) and yang lines (straight). A combination of masculine and feminine lines will create balance.

7. Make provisions for both intense and soft lighting within each room. Lighting can create appropriate atmospheres.

8.   Separate the food preparation area from the front door. Kitchens too close to the front door invite over-indulgence.

9.   Use high ch'i colors like red, purple, fuchsia and russet judiciously in conversation areas. These colors can excite, activate and energize.

10.   Keep your home in optimum condition. Your home's health mirrors your own.

Feng Shui Cures

For every feng shui ill there is a cure so that even an apparent disaster can be changed into something supportive. Some places may require so many cures that they begin to resemble a child who has covered himself with band-aids. Those are places that you might consider leaving. Fortunately, the places that are incurable are in the minority. Most places can be successfully altered.

Use the following information and guidelines to help remedy your living space.

Mirrors

Mirrors remove from view the surfaces they cover. Place mirrors over objects you wish were not there. A wall protrusion or a beam overhead can disappear when its surface is mirrored.

Mirrors reflect a location that cannot be easily seen. A cook who cannot see a kitchen's entrance when standing in front of the stove can hang a mirror on the wall at an angle that reflects the entrance. If you cannot see the entrance door while seated at your work space in your study, hang a mirror on a nearby wall to capture its image.

Mirrors deflect an inauspicious view. When a neighboring structure is perceived to be negative, a mirror hung facing the offending object can redirect the negativity back to the origin.

Plants

Plants connect us to the universe outside. When we dwell in cities or places that aren't blessed with a view of vegetation, we need to be reminded that we are but one segment of the whole picture.

Plants soften hard edges. House plants placed in front of corners, sharp edges of furniture and wall protrusions can temper their potential harm.

Plants bring life to an unused space. An empty corner, a tiny entrance foyer, or a balcony's passageway are spaces that often do not call for furniture. Plants will close the gap from austere to friendly and bring ch'i to these areas.

Plants welcome and infuse life with life. Placed on either side of an entrance door, punctuating our lawns and adorning the sides of our outdoor paths, plants send a message of greeting and an aura of sanctuary to those who enter our domain. Indoors they can bring a breath of life to an area; they are a familiar signpost in any room and can bridge the transition from the unfamiliar to the familiar for any visitor.

Wind

Objects sensitive to wind can amplify beneficial ch'i. The use of windchimes, hanging bells and lightweight curtains can reverberate and amplify beneficial ch'i. I have placed a windchime under the eaves of my home outside the window of my writing room. The tinkling of its metal chimes energizes my mind and spirit when I have been seated at my desk for hours.

Objects sensitive to wind stop racing ch'i. Long narrow hallways that magnify the movement of ch'i can benefit from windchimes hung at strategic points from the ceiling. The ringing or swinging action becomes a pleasant break to the forward motion just as flowers placed in the middle of a footpath slow our pace to our destination.

Water

Water re-unites us with our genesis and bridges the span between our universality and our individuality. Our first connection to life is our experience of water, for life begins by floating in the waters of the womb. Hearing the splash of an indoor fountain or the bubbling waters of a fish tank can be the touchstone for this connection.

Water inspires. The Tao Te Ching states: "True goodness is like water. Water helps the ten thousand things without itself striving...for water is the Way." Contemplating a body of water connects us to the miracle of life's processes.

Water soothes. To gaze upon the surface of water and to hear the sound of its movement brings a feeling of peace.

Color

Color elevates our consciousness. Certain shades of purple, gold, blue or red can dignify and exalt a living space. Blue is the color of meditation and can be appropriate in areas where we need to be self-contained.

Color calms emotions. All colors softened by white slow down our emotional pace. Certain tones of green can soothe a troubled spirit.

Color stimulates ch'i. The color red can activate ch'i and bring attention to an area. The energy that red reflects is considered auspicious, and the selective use of red can bring good fortune.

Color energizes. Use bright colors like red and yellow to stimulate activities and ideas.

Maintenance

Maintenance demonstrates our self-love. Allowing our living space to deteriorate demonstrates a disregard for self. Broken door knobs, windows that won't open, loose planks on a deck or leaky faucets take more energy to ignore than they would to fix.

Changes are facilitated by making thoughtful adjustments in the environment. However, the resolve to change is as important as change itself. A shift in attitude can reroute a life's course. We are inspired by our own actions. Don't worry if you do not have a perfect cure for every situation. It is more important to start down the path of change.

Cures for Common Problems

Problem
A house situated at a T-juncture.

Cure
If the house is at grade level, plant a thick row of hedges or install a fence facing the on-coming street. If the house is raised on pillars, create a wall either with vegetation or any fence material or hang a concave reflective surface or mirror facing the T-juncture. Select a personal lucky symbol and secure it either to the main entrance door or outside in close proximity to the entrance.

Problem
An entrance door facing the wrong direction.

Cure
Place potted plants, red artifacts, sculptures or windchimes on either side of the entrance door. If security is an issue, hang paper or red wood octagon shapes on either side of the door.

Problem
A straight path leading to the house.

Cure
Put a bird bath, bench, trellis, tree or a small pond next to the path closer to the doorway than the beginning of the path.

Problem
Faced with a wall when you enter a home.

Cure
Hang a framed mirror or mirror the entire surface of the wall or install a photograph or painting of a landscape.

Problem
A staircase directly in front of a main entrance door.

Cure
If there's enough room, position a plant or art object so that its

orientation leads one's glance away from the staircase.

Otherwise, hang a wind-sensitive object or bright light in the passage next to the stairway to direct energy to the gathering rooms.

Problem
A long narrow hallway.

Cure
Install high wattage light bulbs in ceiling or stagger wall lights along the length of the hall. As an alternative and if the ceiling is high enough, hang a wind-sensitive object midway down the passage.

Problem
Exposed beams over seating areas, dining tables or beds.

Cure
Attach either a strip of plastic mirror along the entire length of the beam or glue small sections of mirror on the underside of the beam over the place the beam should not be. A beam over a reading chair disappears when a mirror is attached in that location on the beam. Symbols like a personal talisman, a ba-gua (the eight sided symbol of the I Ching) or a wind-sensitive object can undermine a beam's oppression because of the messages they convey. These objects symbolically take the bite out of oppressive ch'i.

Problem
Misaligned doors (opposing doors in a room not in a straight path from each other).

Cure
Hang a mirror or picture next to a door that corresponds with the width of the door opposite.

Problem
A television located near a conversation group seating.

Cure
Drape a piece of cloth over the television or place a plant or screen in front, all of which can easily be moved when the focus in the room is watching television.

Problem
Inappropriate corners or wall protrusions.

Cure
Place a plant in front of a corner or wall protrusion and, if possible, train the leaves to grow upward towards the ceiling.

Problem
Open area dining space.

Cure
Place a screen, a group of plants or a room divider to create a wall separating this from other rooms.

Problem
Not being able to see the entrance to a kitchen while working at the stove.

Cure
Hang a mirror on the wall behind the stove.

Problem
A bath/shower in the same room as the sink and toilet.

Cure
Secure the shower curtain with velcro to the walls, install a lock on the door. If the room is large enough, separate the bath/shower from the sink/toilet with a screen.

Problem
Feeling uneasy when alone in your living space.

Cure
The absence of ch'i in a living space can promote a level of anxiety. To reduce this, keep the house brightly lit, circulate the air with a paddle fan, place a bubbling fish tank in the spot where you feel most vulnerable, or listen to music.

Dare to create the best for yourself and your life's desires will rise into your world like the morning sun.

Chapter Thirteen

Feng Shui Horrors

Our lives do not end at our property lines. The consequences of society's ills seep into our lives, affecting us like toxins dumped into water. Any effort to improve the quality of your life can be diminished if the world around you is at risk. In order to secure personal happiness, we must be involved with changing the current afflictions in society.

To many people, Los Angeles is a city of promise and hope. The ocean waves lap at its shores, the palm trees sway in the breezes and endless sunshine smiles on its residents. Like spices in a well-stocked kitchen, the population's diversity adds dimension and flavor.

Over the years, however, a malignancy has slowly grown, sharply contrasting with the optimistic facade. Freeways, meant to be arteries of progress, have suppressed inexpensive public transportation and have, in fact, become great dividers. Solid concrete paths of racing ch'i criss-cross L.A.'s neighborhoods. Residents have become isolated from one another physically and emotionally by these cement barriers. Like a hangman's noose, freeways have choked the united spirit from this city of angels.

Suburbs were originally designed and built to be the ultimate nesting grounds for the American family. The lives of those in suburbia were expected to parallel the predictability of the carefully laid out straight grids of the roads and the uniformity of lot sizes and homes. But the distance between vision and reality grew as neighborhoods aged, and they were shunned by later generations. Energy does not permeate these neat enclaves of respectability. A drive through suburbia today reveals a still, unpeopled landscape. It is a scene with no balance, and, nothing seems imbued with the energy that flows from human action. No longer do people walk to school, the grocery store or the post office. Sidewalks or pathways that in the past connected people and created a sense of neighborhood have been eliminated as the automobile makes distance inconsequential.

When I was growing up my parents had very little need for baby-sitters because relatives were always close by, available to watch my sister and me while my parents were out. When we played in the neighborhood, we could be seen by those who knew us and were willing to intervene if any situation got out-of-hand. If I ventured too far away from home or was seen roaming around at dinner time, someone was likely to report my whereabouts to mother. Today our neighborhoods have lost their eyes, making us feel alone in a world of many. We have stepped out of the wheel of tao by isolating ourselves in tiny fortresses. In many ways we are deprived of rich life experiences by allowing our society to become blind.

Our world has become smaller as information can be transported anywhere on the globe within a time frame that, 100 years ago, was the stuff of science fiction. Cyberspace is eliminating the need to venture outside our own dwellings. In the not too distant future, we will be able to travel, shop, learn and play via virtual reality. Yet, at the same time, we live in smaller and smaller spaces. Although these developments appear to give us greater flexibility and freedom, they, in fact, exacerbate the individual's feeling of isolation within the community. Feng shui is a new tool to create the underlying structures of cyberspace--relating it to human purpose and community construction. Feng shui helps us connect with those around us even as it reinforces our link to the cosmos since its tools are rooted in a holistic perspective. It gives us a new way to design our planet that can assist in supporting our common goals. Feng shui can be a common language through which we can communicate design. In many ways, feng shui ideas can be effective to help identify directions we should take while offering us a language for description. With this wisdom, we can begin to repair damage from the past and provide a strong foundation to create standards of excellence for the future.

Chapter Fourteen

Your New World

There is no single ideal arrangement for a home. Each family and each member of the household influences the evolution of a living space. Perfection today may be disaster tomorrow. Our lives evolve imperceptibly, and at times we fail to include recent changes with present realities. We must be attuned to the nuances of change in our lives and adjust our world accordingly.

Reaping the benefits of feng shui is not only the province for those who consult a geomancer. The ideas contained in feng shui are simple and are at the core of our intuitive powers. Pure feelings that are allowed to surface are usually in accord with the concepts of feng shui.

Contentment is often derived not from all that we have amassed but from the exquisiteness of each single part. Focusing on improving one area of our lives can lead to satisfaction for the whole. Use feng shui as a guide for adjusting an area, a room or an entire house. You need not change your entire world in a moment. Like learning to speak a foreign language, feng shui becomes easier the longer you practice it.

Feng shui provides the opportunity for positive change through subtle adjustments. Pleats or darts in a dress can transform the mundane into an outfit with flair and style. Subtle chiropractic adjustments can alter the flow of energy throughout a body to produce an extensive physical change. Similarly, slight shifts in a living space can nourish positive change.

When I was a child I would dream of cloud people. I was their queen and would have the power to arrange and rearrange the lives of a whole society that lived in the billowing vapors that floated above my head. When one of my cloud subjects committed a transgression, I would expel him or her to the town's turret. Isolation was their punishment. In a palatial dining hall I sat at the end of the impossibly long dining table. I had the power seat in my kingdom in the clouds. Every room was filled with sun and the rooms' colors changed with the seasons. Summers' rooms were filled witty gay pastels, while the frigid days of winter were spent amid warm dark reds and greens. When I look back on these childhood daydreams, I realize that I already understood that my surroundings could be manipulated to assist me in creating the world I desired. The knowledge that the spaces around us affect us is the basis of feng shui. We need only to uncover our instincts and put them into practice.

Let the river of truth flow through you. Accept its nourishment as it passes. Perfection is yours to absorb. Dreams are not unattainable; they are merely paths we fear to tread. Hold your desires up to the light so that you will never fail to see the way. Use feng shui to assist you in realizing your dreams. Know that you have the power to design your own happiness.